DEDICATION

To the hopeful future of modern man

Cover Design: Michelle Hovde Bastian
Text Layout: Mike Peterson & Michelle Hovde Bastian
Editing: Thanks go to Kris Vilmin, Colin Wilkerson & Mike Downing
for their help
Illustrations: Thanks to Trace P.

Published by Gary Hukriede, Saint Paul, Minnesota USA

ISBN: 978-0-9839965-0-7 Soft Cover

Revised First Edition

Printed and bound in the United States of America

CONTENTS

AUTHOR'S NOTE

HOW THIS CAME ABOUT

I have always been one for observing, questioning, challenging, and taking action. I am constantly observing, analyzing and trying to understand. Throughout my life, whenever I was part of a group, work team, or at events and gatherings, I always silently studied people. During my professional career I have overseen and managed many people.

This writing is based on a lifetime of observation. Every opportunity to watch a group of people is a time to learn. I have observed the interaction of human beings of different cultures, and have been interested in cultures around the world (I did research in West Africa while pursuing my degree), and in subcultures within our American society as well. This is why I decided on a degree in International Relations.

As a working manager, I utilized the study of personality styles to better understand my fellow human beings, as well as for my staff to better understand each other. In this book I examine and relate these personality styles socially and politically. Personality styles relate to everyday life and human interaction. They effect personal interaction in the workplace, within our families, our community and society at large.

I hope by relating personality styles to politics, this book will help the average citizen, who is not concerned with political issues, to break down and examine political ideologies. Persons in the broad middle of the political spectrum will find this book interesting -- those spread politically from center-left to center-right. As you read, keep in mind that the remaining far-left and far-right persons and candidates do not represent the greatest interest of the majority.

I began this book with a neutral political view. Even though I have my own personal views, I tried to be non-partisan while writing. However, as I delved into the two major political poles in our American culture, I found myself slipping to the right-of-center. I do better with facts, details, and data than I do with over-sensitivity and pomp. I do not purposely try to dwell on the liberal psyche, but found it pivotal to our era in which liberalism begun its societal influence decades earlier. One of the premises of this writing is that over the past decades society has done a landslide to the left.

In this text, I use the term *liberal* to distinguish that extreme end of the political left (which I labeled on the bell chart in Chapter One as the "left foot." The extreme opposite foot is labeled the "ultra-conservative foot"). Within these two political extremes are the ranges of political conscience, and where, between the two meridians on the bell chart hovers the greatest mass of society.

I present the range of Republican conservatism from ultra-conservative and Religious Right, to centered moderate-conservative. On the left political spectrum I make a distinction between liberal, liberal-Democrat, and moderate-Democrat. The Democratic Party ranges from liberal sensitivities to moderate-Democrat principles. I have given the term liberal its own identity because it also tends to be the most problematic political psyche in politics and society. Moderate-Democrats are more fiscally aware, and therefore, more tuned-in to the life-blood of our Constitutional Republic – our free-market system and its fiscal responsibility.

I also wrote this book thinking of future youth, to give them a better understanding of our social and political culture earlier in their youth, than I had, to learn about life. This focus is evident in Chapter Ten: "The Decades of Life," and "Men and Women"; these topics are to enlighten young people. I wish to lessen the knowledge gap for future generations. Good advice and knowledge is worth its weight in gold.

A writer must at times ask, "Will what I write be a paradigm for the future?" It is always the plight of those that write about current events and social change that it takes society sometimes many years to accept these new concepts. This book is an attempt to understand the human condition in the context of the four default personality styles. We all have a dominant personality style that is inherent in each of us.

I hope this book will help readers understand personality styles, how they affect individuals and society, and how understanding personality styles can be extended to politics. Some concerns I have proposed in the text are the need for a strong independent third party in America, and to awaken the reader to the importance of individual participation in everyday issues. At every level, this interaction improves daily life, the well-being of fellow citizens, and society at large. To influence or change behavior, one must first recognize and understand the prevailing social conscience and psyche of the day. One is then able to educate and ultimately change minds; and motivate the populous to take action that will cause change.

In summary, what I wish to accomplish is acquaint the reader to personality styles so he or she is better able to understand their fellow man, and to then relate these personality styles to politics. I then delve into the political psyche of the liberal to help the reader better understand the liberal mind.

Throughout the text I have added appropriate sayings by the early founders and other persons. On some issues I have given greater precedence and direct the reader to a related item in the Appendix. I highly recommend the reader to review the information in the Appendix of this book.

> *The thing I find with writing a book is that you never know when you are done.*
>
> *The Author*

IS AMERICA
AT THE BREAKING POINT?

Yes, we did produce a near-perfect republic. But will they keep it? Or will they, in the enjoyment of plenty, lose the memory of freedom? Material abundance without character is the path of destruction.

~ Thomas Jefferson

IS AMERICA AT THE BREAKING POINT?

Introduction to the Four Predominant Personality Styles

WHICH ONE ARE YOU?

The following introduction will help you understand your fellow human being through Personality Styles. It helps answer the many social, cultural, and political questions you have always wondered about. Helping you understand your fellow associates, cultural neighbors, spouse, significant others, relatives, friends, and the political world around you.

PROMOTER, DIRECTOR, SUPPORTER and ANALYTIC*

PROMOTER
Expressive

SUPPORTER
Relater

◀**Aggressive**   **Passive**▶

DIRECTOR
Pragmatic

ANALYTIC
Analytic

The words Promoter, Director, Supporter and Analytic, have evolved to describe the characteristics of each of these styles, and are used interchangeably with other terms to refer to these same characteristic behaviors.

WHAT ARE PERSONALITY STYLES?

Many things are divisible by four. There are four directions, and four seasons to every year. The ancient Greeks believed in four basic elements: wind, sun, water, and soil. As there are four walls that hold a building, and four DNA families from which we all come, so are there four *Personality Styles* that determine our worldview, socially, and politically.

Personality Styles are a means to explain our tendency toward one behavior characteristic over another. In other words, we all have certain repeatable (preprogrammed) dominant characteristics that fall into one of four predominant (default) categories. The tendency to be of a certain personality style appears to be a genetic trait. Personality Styles are the psychological totality of how we think, react, and perceive the world around us. Therefore, genetics and heredity give us our style, but environment, parenting, life experiences and culture also have an effect. However, at the end of the day, each of us still has a default style that is inherent in us. The core default is always there. (I try not to dwell on the social aspects of Personality Styles since we can alter, and we do alter many times in a day, our Personality Style characteristics to match our environment or social situation, suppressing our core default style).

Depending on the industry you are in, the education you have had, or the preference of the individual writer, lecturer, or trainer, you will see these four personality styles referred to by different names. They may be referred to as "Temperament Types, Social Styles, Personality Types, Character Types," or even "Behavior Styles." However they are identified, each of us has a dominant Personality Style. In addition, we also have an *Accent Personality Style*; that is, some characteristics we share with a different Personality Style. Human beings are complex. Everyone adapts their Personality Style according to the social situation. Therefore, although we emulate and react in the characteristics of a particular style, we also have *Associated Styles* in which we also interact. This ability to adapt one's Style to fit the situation is a powerful social tool. In summary, personality styles are a series of consistent actions and behaviors. They are repeated characteristics and behaviors in response to social interaction and stimulus. Personality styles are thought to be a combination, predominantly of genetic inheritance, but also of environmental influence. The root cause of personality styles is hidden within the DNA molecule.

DNA is significant to all living things. We do not know what the future holds, but with genetic engineering, personality styles will ultimately be manipulated from this molecular level (See, "DNA The Code of Life, A brief Overview" in the Appendix).

UNDERSTANDING PERSONALITY STYLES

The concept of Personality Styles is not new. The four styles have been recognized for millenniums and throughout history have been called by different names. As early as Mesopotamian and Egyptian cultures, these four types of human personality were recognized. The Greeks also mentioned them in their literature.

Ancient cultures put these styles into perspective based on daily life. As mentioned earlier, they were referred to as the "Four Seasons," and by the names of common animals chosen for each creature's similarity to the style. They were also compared to the four natural elements, which the world was considered to consist of at the time: earth, air, fire and water. Historically, this ancient study of the four Personality Styles (referred to historically as the "four humours") has survived the test of time, and other than descriptive terms changing through the ages, they have remained.

There are many other methods used to understand Personality Styles, some are very specific and delve more into a psychological perspective. I have chosen to use a simple, basic, and straightforward approach for my explanation. Other models are available from many other sources, and many become rather complex. I opted for less complication, and therefore, a more general study of the subject. Much is still to be gained even at a basic level of introduction.

Learning about Personality Styles some years ago, I could not help but notice how these styles related to other areas, and how things could be predicted based on this information. I was acquainted with learning styles; introverts and extroverts, followers and leaders, liberal and conservative. Personality styles appeared to tie all these things together. Things like personality, culture, nationality, economic status, and political affiliation had related characteristics. Once you are able to understand and identify these personality styles, you are more able to predict outcomes of future events, as well as the demeanor and related characteristics of leaders, spouses, business partners, and associates.

You may have wondered why you get along well with or could work so well with one person and not so well with another. Why is there chemistry between one person and yourself, but not another. Why do people react this way? In any environment where a task needs to be accomplished by a group of persons, there may inherently be conflict. Certain people work better together than others, but we can learn to understand and effectively interact with all. Research has found that certain personality types complement others, while certain personality combinations can be antagonistic. Opposites appear to attract.

One person thinks as a liberal, while another as a conservative. Why does one ethnic group have predominant personality style characteristics, while another is known by different characteristics? Many things can be explained by knowing the basic default each of us lives with; our Personality Style. As individuals have a certain Personality Style, so do many cultures have a collective predominant Style. Some examples: Germany has a concentration of the "Director Style", the United States is "Analytic", while France appears to be "Promoter." How can all these phenomenons occur across a whole culture? These are questions that have plagued mankind for millenniums. It has been identified as stereotype. A more modern understanding has called it Personality Style.

One can easily see Personality Styles at work around them. Understanding Personality Styles promotes a better understanding of fellow human beings and therefore, improves our interaction. Companies train employees in Personality Styles to help improve their interaction as a work group. Knowledge of Personality Styles helps us better understand our customer, so we are better able to interact with them. We are more productive individuals when we work in a field or job that is natural to our Personality Style (such as an Analytic working in accounting). By age twenty your personality style has become consistent. The following are two scenarios showing how personality styles play-out in social settings.

PERSONALITY STYLES: WAITING FOR AN ELEVATOR
If the four Personality Styles were waiting for an elevator, the PROMOTER would talk too much and forget to push the elevator button. The DIRECTOR would push the button many times, getting more impatient the more he has to push it. The SUPPORTER would patiently wait for the elevator to arrive, and the ANALYTIC would step into the elevator, but would immediately step out again because there were too many people in the elevator for which it is posted.

THE PERSONALITY STYLE GOLF GAME
If the four Personality Styles would all go golfing together, the DIRECTOR would play the game no matter what. The ANALYZER would keep score and make sure that all the rules and regulations were followed. The SUPPORTER would drive the cart, make sure everyone was accounted for, and keep the group together. The PROMOTER would never finish the game. The Promoter would only make it to the fifth hole, and then go to the clubhouse to socialize. Happy golfing with Personality Styles!

ANALYSIS OF THE PERSONALITY STYLE CHART
Many things can be concluded simply by looking at the chart. It is obvious extroverts draw their energy and creativity from others. In essence, they need people to draw energy from. Introverts, on the other hand, draw their energy and creativity from within themselves.

From the chart it is observed that Supporters share the same side of the Personality Chart with Promoters, while Analyzers are listed on the opposite side with Director Personality Styles. But diagonally Supporters are compatible with Directors, and Analytics with Promoters. These two polar associations validate the old adage that, "opposites attract." Thus, a Promoter is complemented by an Analyzer, and vice-versa. Consequently, a Director is complimented by a Supporter Personality Style, and vice-versa. As a Director Personality Style, I have experienced this as an employee or participant in a group. I always blend best, and I am better able to work with, and generally feel more comfortable with the Supporter Personality, which compliments me. Together, we easily accomplish tasks.

At the top of the chart you see that both the Promoter and Supporter need structure and guidance. The Promoter gets its structure from the Analytic, while the Supporter is reinforced by the Director. I once asked a strong Promoter Personality what she would do if she were stranded on a remote deserted island in the Pacific. She thought about it for a moment and said, "I would probably die." The same question asked of a Director Personality Style yielded many plans and solutions, in detail.

PERSONALITY STYLE CHART

INFORMAL - PEOPLE ORIENTATED - EXTROVERTED - EMOTIONAL FOCUS - POLITICAL LIBERAL
More disorganized persons

PROMOTER   Expressive aggressive
Free spirit likes to have fun, does not like rules or boredom. Wants attention, recognition, prestige
(otherwise becomes manipulative)
Most liberal. Complemented by the Analytic Personality Style
Has conflict with Director Personality Style
CORE OF LIBERALISM

I. Balloon   II. Exploder

SUPPORTER   Relator passive
Wants everything to be at peace & harmony
Pleasant, patient, likeable, and easy to get along with
People orientated, do not like insensitivity.
(otherwise 'drag their feet' & become passive)
Complemented by the Director Personality Style

I. Superagreeable   II. Staller

DIRECTOR   Pragmatic aggressive
Organized & strong-willed, main focus is task accomplishment
Natural leaders. Express themselves openly & directly.
Respect tradition & justice. Do not like inefficiency and apathy
(otherwise becomes pushy, domineering & stressed)
Most conservative. Complemented by the Supporter
Has conflict with Promoter Personality Style
CORE OF CONSERVATISM

I. Tank   II. Sniper   III. Bull Dozer

ANALYTIC   Analytic passive
They like everything in order and at peace
Do not like spontaneity, being wrong, or caught without details
(otherwise become withdrawn)
Complemented by the Promoter Personality Style

I. No People   II. Chronic-complainer

< Aggressive
dominant

< SOCIAL >
< ASSERTIVENESS >

Passive >
easygoing

FORMAL - TASK ORIENTATED - INTROVERTED - FACT & DETAIL FOCUS - POLITICAL CONSERVATIVE
More organized persons

THE PROMOTER

The major goals of the Promoter personality are to have fun and bring thrills and action into the routine of life. Promoters are very emotional and display expressive-aggressive social assertiveness. Other names for the Promoter Personality Style are: EXPRESSIVE, SOCIALIZER, ENTERTAINER and ADVENTURER.

Strengths	Challenges
Motivating, enjoyable to be around	Disorganized, procrastinates & too flexible
High energy & competitive	Risk taker & have too much going on at once
Creative & imaginative	Lack concern for detail, follow-up & conviction
Adventuresome & very outgoing	Do not like data or rules
Quick decision-makers	Limited attention span, loses interest easily
Good communicators	Appear egotistical to others & vie for attention
Very persuasive & confident	Very emotional & may exaggerate
Intuitive	Set unrealistic goals & are dreamers
Like challenges	Seek approval & need compliments
Like to be physically fit	Dislike isolation or being left out

Persons of the Promoter Personality Style can be described as very outgoing and free spirited; they enjoy life to the fullest. They like change, challenges, action, excitement and adventure, and the freedom to enjoy life without being bound by rules and regulations. They are energetic and want to be "where the action is." To them, the present moment is the most important – yesterday is easily forgotten and tomorrow is not relevant. Because of this, they tend to be short-sighted. Promoters are very active and like to be physically fit. Born entertainers, they are full of fun and mischief. To them variety is the spice of life. Challenges, risk taking, and toys are an important part of their action filled world. Promoters are willing to try anything, especially if it will give them pleasure or a good time. However, they do not always consider the consequences. Promoters are easily tempted and have little foresight for future saving or conserving. Promoters like the better things in life like good food, entertainment, the latest fashions and events.

In a work environment, Promoters are very motivated with high energy (as long as the job is still new and exciting), but will never become totally absorbed by their work. When they have a purpose, they put all their energy into it. They are creative and spontaneous, and at times of crisis they are at their best. But Promoters are easily bored and tire of the routine and want to move on to new adventures and excitement. They would do poorly on an assembly-line type of job. Because they put so much energy initially into a job or project, they burn out quickly. They hate indecisiveness in others and too much data. Innovative and good at generating ideas, Promoters usually lose interest before they are able to see their ideas through to completion. Promoters are seen as overly talkative and social, dramatic, impulsive, and manipulative. They make quick decisions based on emotion, not data, and tend to put off worries and concerns as long as possible.

Usually enthusiastic and confident, Promoters are positive and optimistic and always look to the bright side. They love attention and pomp; limelight and identity are very important to the Promoter Personality Style. This explains why so many Promoters are actors/ actresses, entertainers, and comedians, lifestyles well-suited to that of Hollywood. Promoters need change, and they wish to live a carefree life where everyone is happy and enjoying themselves.

Promoters are very sociable and trusting of others, they are likeable and enjoyable to be around. They can be very charming and convincing. Because they are very extroverted, they easily initiate relationships and seek others for their own interaction. Since they are good at influencing and motivating others, they are natural born sales people who get others involved. It has been shown that Promoters have a tendency to increase the blood pressure of others around them. They are very intuitive which is paralleled with their sensitivity. Promoters are very verbal, and do not hold anything in, but they can become manipulative if things do not go their way. They usually have too much going on at once and burn out quickly, therefore they may move on, leaving the responsibility for others. Many are hyperactive, and as such, may suffer from fatigue, exhaustion, or even ulcers.

Promoters usually watch their diet and try to stay in good physical shape. They may obsess over grooming and the latest clothing styles. They enjoy the outdoors and are very environmentally conscious. Nature gives the Promoter a calming effect and relaxation that they are unable to find elsewhere in society. Therefore, they are very protective of natural areas, and consider environmental protection over that of the economy -- such as, being against drilling for oil to reduce energy costs, even during tough economic times.

Promoters live in an emotional world where they are either on top of the world or in the dumps. They are high strung and excite easily; they may change their mood quickly and can be short fused, but their outbursts are usually short lived. They love to shop and spend money freely and are collectors of many things. In relationships, Promoters are intuitive to the feelings of others, but may be reluctant to commit, and it is difficult for them to handle being hurt or rejected. If rejected, they take flight. They can be vocal and outspoken, and because they are very emotional and do not rely on details, Promoters tend to be illogical and compulsive at times and tend to have deep-seated envy. They can be devious and quick to deny when they do not get their way or when a situation goes badly.

Professions where you would find Promoters are sales people, actors and actresses, politicians, and marketing where they can use their creativity.

Hollywood is full of Promoter Personality Styles. Many actors and actresses are Promoter personalities. Acting fits the characteristics and needs of the Promoter. Since the Hollywood psyche began, there have been media reports of Hollywood divorces, excesses, extravagance in living and spending, drugs, and premature deaths due to accidents and excessiveness. Hollywood is truly a Promoter's paradise, it fits the Promoter well: the spotlight, the attention, the prestige and recognition. Actors are able to make big money they can spend freely. Movie stars tend to deify themselves more than any other group. No other industry has so many awards programs. This is very characteristic of the Promoter Personality.

Some examples of persons having the Promoter Personality Style are: Politically: former President Bill Clinton, Boris Yeltsin (former Russian Premier), and Arnold Schwarzenegger; Explorers: Amelia Earhart and Chuck Yaeger; Entertainers and Performers: Elvis Presley, Robin Williams, Tom Cruise, Liza Minelli, Eddie Murphy, Whoopi Goldberg, and Paris Hilton. Television reporters and late night hosts: Geraldo, and the late Johnny Carson.

In observation, cultural groups as the Semitics and African-Americans, the Irish, French, and Australians, appear to manifest the Promoter Personality Style.

I have worked with many sales representatives in the business community. When they walk into your facility, they are filled with excitement, vibrating with ambition, and totally immersed in their own agenda for the day. Once ready, they go off to their first appointment with energy, excitement, and enthusiasm to make a big sale, which fulfills their need for competition and challenge. When they come into your business, they expect your full attention whether you are in the middle of a project or have a tight schedule that day. They are self-absorbed and totally focused on their own projects.

By early afternoon they have exhausted their energy, and the days' work is no longer fun or exciting for them. It is no wonder that salespeople change jobs often. They become bored with the routine and the excitement of a new job can wear off quickly for them. They must renew this excitement again and again to fulfill their Promoter characteristics. I have experienced this personality style many times in my dealings and travels with sales representatives. Although Promoters may make a very good income in sales or related positions, they tend to spend money freely, and by frequent job-jumping they limit building a future nest-egg.

Whether you are in a relationship or interacting with a Promoter co-worker, they need structure and direction. Tell them what you want, draw out answers, and let them talk. Avoid too many details. Promoters cannot tolerate boredom, details, or indecisiveness. As mentioned earlier, it is not uncommon for a Promoter salesperson to jump from company to company, job to job, every so many years because of their need for change and excitement, craving attention, recognition, and prestige. If they do not receive these on the job or in a relationship, they can become manipulative or take flight. Because of their nature, Promoters are susceptible to chemical dependency. They would benefit from slowing down, analyzing more, and utilizing organization and follow-through. Promoters have a natural conflict with the Director Personality Style.

THE DIRECTOR

The main goals of the Director are task accomplishment, results, and control. They are natural leaders. Other names given to the Director Personality Style are: PRAGMATIC, DRIVER, CONTROLLER, BUILDER, AGGRESSIVE and RULER.

Strengths

Initiates, takes charge & gets results
Organized, responsible & innovative
Born leaders, they zero in on others
Forward looking & fast decision makers
Strong willed, dedicated & practical
Approaches problems directly
Task & results orientated

Challenges

Autocratic & blunt
Only a bottom-line perspective
Sometimes toy with people
Workaholics, high energy & too competitive
May overlook other's ideas & suggestions
Impatient
Opinionated

Persons with a Director Personality Style are very responsible, practical, self-assured and results oriented. Natural leaders, they are comfortable with authority and command. Directors take charge, initiate activities, and delegate. They are good decision makers with a bottom-line perspective and want to see results. Self-motivated and disciplined, they control themselves and others. Strong willed, pragmatic, and dedicated, Directors tend to be workaholics. They are organized, forward thinking, assertive, and express themselves openly and directly. Directors are vocal, direct, and may readily confront others.

Directors have deep respect for traditions and justice. They believe in preparation, saving, and building on a solid foundation. Directors are usually strong willed and organized. They desire respect, and have an appreciation for maintaining the status quo. Directors are perceptive and efficient managers and problem solvers, and utilize people in their best capabilities. A Director is a bottom-line results person who seeks to achieve tasks and accomplishments by focusing on reality and facts. They function best in a traditional, hierarchic structure. Directors are decisive, and at times demanding.

Director Personality Styles are more emotionally reserved, but good at focusing on others. They are more formal and matter-of-fact in their dealings with others. Comfortable with being by themselves, they are independent and accept change, and some risk, but with caution. They want to know, as much as possible, up front how things will work out. Directors want results and to be successful in their goals and responsibilities. They are competitive and determined, and like to take credit for their accomplishments.

Directors are self-motivated, forward looking, task accomplishers. They provide drive, direction, and momentum to a work group, project, or process. Self disciplined, they become impatient if projects do not proceed steadily. They do not do well with persons who lack a sense of urgency and dedication to their job, or who are overly emotional or sensitive. These interactions make Directors stressed, pushy, and demanding. They may also be argumentive.

Because of their propensity for task accomplishment, job completion, and bottom line perspective, Directors tend to have tension and stress related health problems. They tend to rush and eat too fast. Directors are also at high risk for chemical dependency and physical ailments related to stress and tension. Directors would gain if they had more empathy and tolerance for other people and employees, and took time to understand the feelings and concerns of others.

Common professions of Directors are in positions of leadership, authority and responsibility. Many become supervisors and managers in business. Some examples of persons with the Director Personality Style are: Generals Patton (WW II) and Schwarzkopf (1991 Dessert Storm invasion); Heads of State: President Ronald Reagan, Margaret Thatcher and Golda Meir, and former Senator Hillary Clinton; Media anchors: Ted Koppel and Rush Limbaugh; Business executives: Lee Iacocca and H. Ross Perot.

When interacting with a Director Personality Style, be specific in your interaction, communicate in a down-to-earth manner and get to the point, do not waste their time. In a personal relationship, a Director wants to know up front what you want out of the relationship. Uncomfortable showing personal feelings, they may maintain a business-like relationship and tend to want to control the relationship. Directors are either on top the world, or down in the dumps. If rejected, Directors do not have much forgiveness, and may seek revenge. They are also manipulative at times; this is a shared characteristic with the Promoter Personality.

THE SUPPORTER

The main goals of the Supporter are to have stability and things at peace. Other names used to describe the Supporter Personality Style are: RELATER, AMIABLE, DO-GOODER, CLIMATE BUILDER.

Strengths
Friendly, easy to know & sensitive
Keep peace & harmony
Good at reconciling conflicts & friction
Dedicated, loyal & stable
Good listeners, patient & sympathetic
People & relationship oriented
Create a positive environment
Sets high standards
Always willing to help & asks questions
Easily blend into situations & work groups
Culturally orientated

Challenges
Procrastinators & resistant to change
Unassertive & too accepting
Dislike risk & pressure
Not focused on results, overlook details
Vulnerable & very sensitive
Accept inconvenience to keep peace
Avoid conflict
At times may seem wishy-washy
Struggle with making crucial decisions
Need reassurance
They are followers

Persons who are a Supporter Personality Style are responsive to other's needs. They are amiable, sincere, congenial, and liked by others. Because they are easygoing, understanding, friendly and pleasant, they are easy to be around. Supporters have a positive approach to life and generally seem relaxed. Because of their passive, non-conflictive nature, they are sometimes referred to as *do-gooders* or *peacemakers*, and seek harmony through common goals. As the name implies, Supporters are very loyal and supportive people. They usually shy away from the spotlight, and feel rewarded when they are able to help others fulfill their goals and needs. Supporters like familiarity and do not do well with insensitive and pushy people, or impersonal details and hard facts.

Supporters are good listeners and mediators, and enjoy communicating and socializing. They do best in a non-threatening and friendly environment. Supporters avoid confrontation and conflict. Instead, they try to keep peace and harmony, and are careful not to cause conflicts themselves. They will tolerate inconvenience just to keep peace. Team players and easily managed, Supporters tend to be the "glue" of the organization, holding everyone together. They like nature and outdoor activities, such as camping.

Supporters do not often stand up for themselves; instead, they share people's concerns. They try to maintain harmony, and are environmentally conscious, which are both in sync with the Promoter Personality Style. However, Supporters are also at odds with the

Promoter because of the Promoters lack of structure and non-direction, and because of their flightiness. Instead, they look to the Director to offset their need for direction, organization, structure and decision making. Respectful of authority, Supporters prefer to follow than to lead, and they easily rely on others. Supporters will assist a Director with a project or duty without the need for the recognition that the Director relishes.

As employees, Supporters are easily supervised and directed; they are dedicated, dependable, stable, and trusting. Supporters are behind-the-scenes people, but if put in a role of authority, they are able to lead, but lead with more of an emphasis on employee feelings, than task accomplishment. They look to the Director Personality Style for direction and organization. Very supportive and considerate of others, they forgive easily and blame themselves when things go wrong. If they are hurt, Supporters tend to put up a wall. Supporters also tend to be procrastinators. Since feelings are crucial to the Supporter, their judgment is usually based, first on people, then on the facts and task. They also tend to give in to other's needs.

Some common professions of Supporters are positions involving limited confrontation, helping people, and in support positions. Jobs in healthcare, education, the environment, social services would be good matches for a Supporter Personality Style. Some examples of persons having the Supporter Style are Entertainers: Bill Cosby, Stevie Wonder, and Paul McCartney; Television show hosts: Larry King, Oprah Winfrey, Jay Leno, Ed McMahon; Actors: Michael J. Fox, Lucille Ball, Desi Arnez, Bob Newhart; Sports: Michael Jordan; Humanitarian: Mother Theresa; and former First Lady Nancy Reagan.

In personal interactions and as employees, Supporters have a sense of dedication and commitment, and are very dependable. They are loyal, committed team members, and have good perseverance, but would benefit more by being results oriented and focused more on task completion.

Supporters would function more effectively by asserting themselves and asking more of others. They are too accepting and avoid any confrontation with others. They are deep thinkers, so they may dwell on some negative experience for a long period. At times they appear to others as being wishy-washy and too laid back. In a relationship, they tend to blame themselves when things do not work out. Because of their easy, relaxed nature, Supporters tend to suffer from fewer medical problems. They have the least anxiety and have a concern for good health.

When interacting with a Supporter, do not be pushy. Avoid conflict and be a patient and good listener to their concerns. Establish a relationship and have an honest dialogue to draw out their thoughts, issues, and concerns. Show your personal interest and concern in them; ask for their agreement, ideas, and help towards goals. Minimize their risk and gently explore areas where there is disagreement.

THE ANALYTIC

The main goals of the Analytic are order, respect, and for everyone to get along. Other names for the Analytic Personality Style are: PLANNER, ANALYZER, THINKER, THE COMPUTER.

Strengths	Challenges
Methodical, thorough & organized	*Procrastination & appear aloof*
Rational, thinkers & respect knowledge	*Take too long to make decisions*
Obtain all needed information	*Need too much data*
Maintain accuracy & standards	*Overemphasize data & details*
Conscientious, courteous & patient	*Avoid confrontation & conflict*
Good budgeters, planners & persistent	*Perfectionists, too structured*
Finds the best solution, logical	*May overlook feelings or values*

Persons who have an Analytic Personality Style are responsible and results oriented. They are very logical and orderly, use good reasoning, and are comfortable with high standards and exactness. They are fact finders, innovators, planners and budgeters. Thinkers by nature, Analytics have an affinity for logic and knowledge. Very organized, they strive to live in a structured world, with the philosophy that life should follow a logical order. Very cautious, systematic and thorough, they are an anchor of reality. In a work environment especially, the Analytic Personality Style provides stability and structure. Analytics generally have good moral principles and values, and are thrifty and cautious throughout their life.

Analytics are predictable, competent, understanding, conscientious, diplomatic, courteous, and caring. Analyzers are disciplined and strive for accuracy and perfection. They analyze the world around them; they analyze people and the nature of people's intent and actions. In this respect, Analytics have a similarity with the Director Personality. But Analytics are complemented by the Promoter Personality Style.

To Analytics, all underlying details are important and everything should be brought into consideration before making a final decision. To an Analytic, it is just as important how you get to a solution or goal (the process) as the end result itself. They like to plan ways of doing things better, especially in the workplace. Analytics want to understand causes, and are critical of the results until things work correctly. Comfortable with detailed tasks, they define and clarify information, data and details. This makes Analytics a good match for research.

Analytics are good at budgeting time and money. They want to have things planned out and be able to predict with reason and assurance, their future plans or results. Analytics maintain standards and honesty, and are comfortable with rules. Analytics are turned off by hype, manipulation and excitement, without tangible details or reason. Although they provide structure for the Promoter, this is where Analytics differ with Promoters. Analytics do not buy into the pure emotion and hype without the basis of facts or details. The saying, "steady as she goes", fits the Analytic well. They are steady in their actions and are usually serious with little surface emotion.

Analytics maintain a deep emotion but seldom show it. Once upset, they never forget. They are difficult people to read, but expect you to understand them. Because of their commitment, they will stay in a relationship a long time, even with adversity. But once they change their mind, it is final. They are "true blue" loyal friends. Analytics usually stay at a job a long time. Depending on the personality and demeanor of a supervisor, Analytics may have reservation toward or mistrust of authority.

Analytics are very self-controlled, orderly and precise, and because all information, details and data must be considered before making a decision, it can take them a long time to make a final decision. They must be objective, and define and clarify data before they make a final decision. Once the decision has been made, it is final. Analytics stick to their principles, opinions and projects. When challenged, they become even more determined. Many times this is viewed by others as being stubborn. Analytics are very capable and deliberate; if given a project, it gets done. In this respect, they are anchors of reality in any social interaction or in the work place.

Common professions where Analytics do well are engineering, science, computer analysts, accountants, and statisticians. Analytics would be matched well with any field where details, specific data, and exacting measurement are required. In comparison, the Promoter Personality Style is at its best during crises, but the Analytic is at their best only when they have prepared and are immersed in data and details. Some examples of persons who are Analytic Personality Style are: Political: Former Vice-President Al Gore; Military leader: General Colin Powell; Television night time host: David Letterman; Author: William F. Buckley Jr.; Sports: Tom Landry (football player & famous NFL coach); Scientists: Thomas Edison, Madame Curie (discovered Radium), Albert Einstein; Actors: David Carradine and Kevin Costner, Katherine Hepburn and the criminal investigator/literary character of Sherlock Holmes.

When interacting with an Analytic Personality Style, build an environment where free discussion and sharing of ideas is accepted. When instituting a project with an Analytic, first source the necessary facts and details related to the project. Then clearly define the goals and tasks involved, and provide your commitment and assurance of follow through to its completion. Analytics are very predictable, but uncomfortable with spontaneity.

Others perceive Analytics as being too cautious, overly structured and following "the book" too much. Analytics try to be more fun and outgoing, and periodically try to break from their mold, but quickly return to its security. Analytics should not be pushed into a decision without first letting them sort out all the details and facts. When working with an Analytic, thoroughly outline each step of the process, in some cases limit the choices and decisions they need to make to expedite the project.

Analytics could improve their interaction with others, especially in a team environment, if they were more spontaneous, more open to risks and less data and detail driven. They may focus on the details so much that they lose sight of the "big picture". In essence, "they do not see the forest for the trees". Health-wise, Analytics are more susceptible to ulcers and nervous conditions because they hold everything in. They also tend to be hypochondriacs because of their overt attention to detail.

In summary, although the Promoter and Director may be at odds socially and politically, they share several characteristics in common. Both have energy and drive and like personal acknowledgement. Each believes in strong personal convictions. Directors and Analytics share task orientation, rely more on detail and fact than hearsay and hype, and both are structured and organized. The Supporter and Analytic also have shared characteristics. Both are pacifists, they avoid conflict, and strive to keep order and harmony. Sometimes, if rejected, Supporters may temporarily seek the Promoter's "Freedom of Flight" world, but soon return to a more stable environment such as what the Analytic or Director provides.

The following pages are listed a quick reference chart for Personality Style characteristics. To determine your Personality Style, see the form, "Quick Method To Determine Your Personality & Associate Style" in the beginning of the Appendix.

PERSONALITY STYLE MATRIX
How to better understand your fellow human beings

	PROMOTER	DIRECTOR	SUPPORTER	ANALYTIC
Behavior Characteristics:	Creative, warm, energetic, good verbal skills, influential, persuasive, good salesperson, may at times be challenging, skeptical, or amused, may tune out, but alert when they disagree, craves center of attention, usually optimistic, people focused, fun to be around, initiates relationships	Controls, dictates, is very direct, quick to express agreement or disagreement, straight forward on issues, matter-of-fact, energetic, have bottom-line perspective, disciplined	Agreeable, personable, friendly, caring, helpful, usually attentive, receptive, gives good communicative feedback & eye contact, do not take risks, seek relationships, wish to live & function in harmony, they are usually positive, set good standards, <u>keeps peace</u>	Attentive to detail, patient, systematic, predictable, calm, hard to read, does not give feedback, studious, organized, disciplined, very careful, controlled, maintains standards, needs a lot of data before decision is made
Strengths:	Creativity, persuasive, people-focused, optimistic, good verbal skills, motivating, competitive	Task completion, decisive, gets things done, self-confident, simplifies, provides direction & organization	Likeable, loyal team player, patient, steadfast, supports & encourages others, is dependable, dedicated	Accurate, precise, logical, objective, persistent, fact finders, consciencious, organized
Negatives:	Limited attention, skeptical, at times may be probing, disorganized, argumentive, seems egotistical, lacks follow-through, seems flaky	At times may be domineering, intimidating, alienates others, expresses strong opinion, may feel superior	May be inquiring, at times be disappointed or resentful, indecisive, may waste time, are guilable, they withhold negatives	At times stubborn, seem aloof, procrastinate, unimaginative, boring, make decisions slowly
Likes:	Intellectual, theorectical debate without specific details, likes to be center of attention, communicative, interactive	Bottom-line, brief, direct discussion, expert opinion, relevant examples	Harmony, good feelings, people, others problems, positive social aspect, like predictability, belonging	Structured, logical analysis of issues & details, wants consistency, status quo, preparedness, order, security
Dislikes:	Repetition, simplistic or superficial talk or interaction, indecisiveness, boring data	Impractical, overly sensitive, emotional, long-winded talk, lack a of sense of urgency	Technical, insensitivity, pushy, unfeeling, dehumanizing, people & talk, conflict, taking risks	Hype, poor data & examples, propaganda with little fact, aimless talk, irrelevant humor

	PROMOTER	DIRECTOR	SUPPORTER	ANALYTIC
Needs to feel:	Acknowledged, to be in the limelight & be popular, seeks social recognition & good feeling	Successful, in control, have authority, to be right	Appreciated, trusted, have security, belonging, please others	Capable, ordered, security, controlled environment, independence
When upset or stressed:	Pokes fun at you, may be sarcastic, talks louder/faster, becomes argumentive	Becomes agitated, upset, may yell, blow-up, throw a fit, be sarcastic, derogatory, arrogant	Appears hurt, resentful, submit, accommodates, may be passive-aggressive	Becomes silent, withdraws, takes flight, becomes autocratic
Would benefit by:	Analyzing the data, slowing down, making effort to follow through	Would benefit by being more aware of feelings, practice tolerance toward others	Would benefit by being more task orientated, demand more from others	Would benefit by taking more risk, be less dependent on data, be more exciting & interactive
How to interact successfully with the Personality Style:	Ask specific questions, listen for underlying motives, test their interest, let them talk & listen to their ideas, use flexibility, visual examples, demonstrations, settle for the practical, be enthusiastic	Be brief, get to the point, respond quickly with a plan or course of action, use facts & expertise, be firm, be business-like, task focused	Be casual, sincere, slow down, listen, understand their expectations, ask for their help, get their agreement, set goals, avoid conflict, emphasize self-development	Do your homework, give them time to decide, their lack of response does not mean disagreement, use facts, logic & structure, proceed step-by-step, tie new ideas to old ones
Words associated with each Personality Style:	Artistic, manic, impulsive, changeable, innovative, lively, talkative, carefree, outgoing, perceiving, playful, probing, spontaneous	Economic, industrious, sober, reserved, quiet, rigid, guarded, traditional, depressive, hoarding, judging, scheduling, sensible, judicious	Optimistic, religious, feeling, oversentive, restless, friendly, inspiring, impulsive, fervent, passonate, doctrinarian, receptive, exciteable, intuitive	Theoretical, curious, calm, skeptical, insenitive, careful, marketing, controlled, tough-minded, thoughtful, thinking, reliable, ingenius, theoretical

29

EXPLAINING SOCIETY THROUGH PERSONALITY STYLES

As you have learned, each of us is born with one of four Personality Styles. Over many generations, whole societies and nations have developed a characteristic Personality Style. Only in recent times has such a great intermingling occurred between different cultures on a global basis. Prior to the last 150 years, people were separated by mountains, oceans, or by distance. And therefore, a certain Personality Style became more predominant in one society than another.

For instance, the Asian cultures are generally understood to be Analytic. This personal characteristic has transcended into an entire culture. On the other hand, Germans are thought of as Director Style; taking charge, doing it right, and getting the job done. The French have more of a Promoter Personality Style. Travelers have commented that when traveling from France to Germany, in France it was not as neat (i.e., litter on the streets and individual yards not as tidy), compared to when you enter into Germany. This is reflective of the Promoter (for France), and Director (for Germany), two different Personality Styles with each having a different set of characteristics defining their style.

ASSOCIATE PERSONALITY STYLES

Few of the billions of people on earth are one hundred percent a single Personality Style. Human beings are complex, although each of us falls in a particular repeated default Personality Style, each style is also associated with an *Associate Personality Style*.

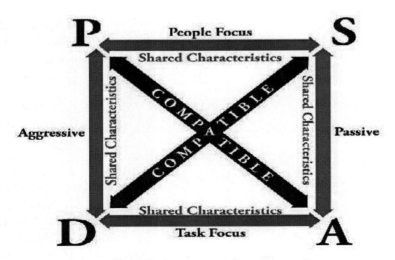

Personality Style Chart – Shared Similarities

As the chart to the left illustrates, there are shared characteristics between Personality Styles. A person may be predominantly of Director Style, but also have detail and analytic skills similar to an Analytic Personality Style. Therefore, that person would lie in a line between the Director and Analytic styles. The strongest characteristics are shared between opposites. There is a strong compatible attraction between the Director and Supporter Personality Styles. Similarly, there is an attraction between the Promoter and Analytic Styles. Therefore, even though we have a dominant Personality Style, throughout the day we react in ways characteristic of other personality styles, but we always return (default) back to our dominant Personality Style.

DEVIATIONS WITHIN A PERSONALITY STYLE

Human beings are complex, and variations that tend to be negative characteristics occur periodically throughout the population. They can only be described as deviations within each of the four predominant Personality Styles. Unless understood and dealt with as a parent, supervisor, team leader, organizer or manager, they can be quite complicating to the completion of tasks, goals, projects, and social interaction. If not intelligently dealt with, these deviant characteristics can jeopardize social interaction, and projects in a work environment.

These are the behaviors that plague supervisors and managers throughout the workforce. They are the deviant Personality Styles that cause most of the greatest conflict for team goals and tasks, and interpersonal conflicts.

Each personality style has subclass deviations. Under the Promoter Personality Style are *The Balloon* and *The Exploder*. With the Director Personality there are *The Tank, Bulldozer,* and the *Sniper*. The Supporter has the *Super-Agreeable*, and the *Staller*. The Analytic has the *No-People* and the *Chronic Complainer.**

These terms have evolved to describe various associated behaviors; these same behavioral characteristics may be referred to by other names.

DEVIATIONS WITHIN THE PROMOTER PERSONALITY STYLE

THE BALLOON is an expressive "know-it-all." Balloons do not really know what they are talking about, but they can be very convincing. In a corporate, social, or political environment a Balloon can sway a decision or idea. When interacting with a Balloon, do not "inhale the hot air", do not get pulled into their psyche. State facts using "I" statements, but provide a face-saving escape for them. Scrap any of their ideas or projects that are unworkable without "blowing their cover."

THE EXPLODER is an expressive aggressive personality that seeks recognition. If they do not get recognition, they may have an emotional outburst. When in their explosive mode, help them regain their control by getting their attention by repeating their name. Show them your concern about their thoughts, ideas or project, then have a "time out."

To avoid future outbursts, learn what sets them off. Review previous outbursts to know what buzz word, or behavior, set them off.

DEVIATIONS WITHIN THE DIRECTOR PERSONALITY STYLE

THE TANK, also referred to as "The Bully", is a pragmatic dictator. Unpredictable, Tanks are abrupt, easily angered, intimidating, and quick to attack on a personal level. Tanks believe their ideas are superior. They do not like change. When working or interacting with a Tank, do not take the Tank's outbursts personally. Stand your ground and control your emotions, but do not try to avoid them. Stand up to a Tank, but do not fight with them. After an interaction, give a Tank time to cool down, acknowledge their ego, and get them to listen. If necessary, firmly interrupt them by saying their name, then compete assertively (not aggressively) with them. Do not argue or speak from your opinion, disagree tactfully. If they continue to interrupt, tell them they are interrupting. Once you have broken through the Tank's defense and they realize that you too only want to accomplish the same goal, be ready to be friendly and the Tank will ally with you. If two Tanks are in conflict, they will fight until one gives in. If evenly matched and neither gives in, they will settle on common ground.

THE SNIPER is a pragmatic aggressive. Snipers throw rocks hidden in snow balls, they attack from behind, and jab you with words while using social constraints as a protective hedge. They build allies and try to sway other persons in a work group to their own philosophies, knowing there is power in numbers. Snipers are very communicative and shy away from authority. Deceitful by nature, they are more comfortable "stirring the pot", and then hiding in a bush to observe how effective their efforts were. Throughout the day, they seem to have accomplished little work.

When interacting with a Sniper, catch them in the act and confront them, but expect denial. Surface the Snipers grievances and deal with them. Get the Sniper "out of the tree" by drawing attention to their grievances with open-ended questions. Seek group opinion, and deal with the issues, and provide them an escape. To prevent future Sniper attacks, provide a regular forum for grievances to be heard. Be aware of the damage they can do. You should never agree with them or become their buddy, and do not expect them to change.

THE BULLDOZER is a pragmatic "know-it-all." Ironically, they do seem to know what is right. When interacting with a Bulldozer, try to coerce them to consider other points of view so others are able to have their say. When interacting with a Bulldozer, educate yourself first on all the details related to a project or issue. Listen and acknowledge the Bulldozers' ideas, and ask "What if..." statements, and clarifying questions such as, "What about two years from now...?" Be cautious not to become a Bulldozer yourself. As a last resort, let a Bulldozer be the expert by allowing them the expertise in a particular area – let them share their knowledge.

DEVIATIONS WITHIN THE SUPPORTER PERSONALITY STYLE

THE SUPER-AGREEABLE is a passive relater, a "yes-person." The Super-Agreeable wants your approval, so they agree with you. When interacting with a Super-Agreeable, make it safe for them to be honest. Then reinforce your relationship with them for an honest dialogue. Then problem solve the issues, reassure them about their involvement and input, and establish a plan to go forward. Ensure their commitment. Do ongoing follow ups to keep the project moving and to keep them motivated.

THE STALLER is a passive relater who feels it is safer to do nothing when faced with a project or duty. The Staller is concerned with hurting someone. They postpone decisions until it is too late, and they promise to do something but nothing ever gets done. When interacting with a Staller, make the environment safe for them to be honest then have an honest dialogue with them, asking pertinent questions. Continue to reassure them about their role and purpose in the project or task, then problem solve issues. If the concerns are about you personally, acknowledge the problem(s), state any relevant information, and then propose a plan.

If it does not involve you, help examine the issues or concerns in question. Prioritize alternatives based on your data or understanding. Continue your support after a decision has been made. Try to keep the action steps in your control, but be aware of Staller overload. To ensure commitment, consistently follow up, and be attuned to any indirect comments or feedback.

DEVIATIONS WITHIN THE ANALYTIC PERSONALITY STYLE

THE NO-PERSON is an analytic passive person who is very negative. They may have had an early disappointment in life, so they continually protect themselves and others from any further disappointment.

When interacting with a No-Person, avoid being dragged into their philosophy of life. Present the negatives first then suggest how to overcome them. Use another person (third party) as a resource for constructive criticism for a project or process. Do not defend a No-Person, analyze their concerns, then problem solve with them, but always be ready to take action on your own to keep the project moving.

THE CHRONIC COMPLAINER is an analytic passive that sees realistically how things could be but feels powerless to change them. Chronic Complainers usually have good insight and see themselves as perfect. Acknowledge what they say, but you may have to interrupt them to bring out strategic points. Do not agree with them. With any project or process, try to get the Chronic Complainer to switch to problem solving. Discuss the main points with them and ask for specifics, then assign limited tasks and set time limits, follow up often.

When it involves another person, triangulate with the Chronic Complainer, the third party, and yourself. Utilize leading questions, such as: "Have you told them (the third party)?" "Can I tell them your concerns?" "I would be happy to set up a meeting." Reinforce to the Chronic Complainer, that if he or she changes their mind, to immediately let you know. When interacting with a Chronic Complainer, try to "beat them to the punch!" Do not become their buddy or reinforce their complaints by being overly nice, taking extra time to listen to them, or give reinforcing body language (nodding head, full attention, etc.). Be consistent and make sure they have some personal responsibility committed to help solve the issue or concern.

CHAPTER ONE

SOCIAL ISSUES and PERSONALITY STYLES

It is only when the people become ignorant and corrupt, when they degenerate into a populace, that they are incapable of exercising their sovereignty. Usurpation is then an easy attainment, and a usurper soon found. The people themselves become the willing instruments of their own debasement and ruin.
~ James Monroe

AMERICA THE GREAT SOCIETY

Americus, the 16th Century map maker of the New World, never conceived that his name would be applied to the greatest democratic experience in all of history. Despite the mix of cultures and nationalities that have come, and continue to come to America to settle in peace and freedom, they are all Americans, and must stand up for the principles of America.

In the United States we have a truly free society. All the options and choices are there for anyone, as long as they abide by the law. One may be overly expressive in this society, but society tolerates our differences; it believes that everyone should have an opportunity to speak. However, there is a line of toleration, which in comparison to other societies in the world, is still a rather wide line of tolerance. If that line is crossed, the laws of the land will hold the violator responsible.

With all its cultural diversity, America is a melting pot. First it was the English, then the Germans, then Scandinavians who were followed by other groups. America keeps cooking a diverse ethnic stew. It has always been the land of opportunity and economy, and therefore groups from around the world have immigrated to its shores for a better economic and political life.

Regardless of the social diversity, politically, all persons fall into one ideology or another. The chart below illustrates this diverse political spectrum.

POLITICAL IDEOLOGIES

LIBERAL	INDEPENDENT	REPUBLICAN
ULTRA-LIBERAL	MODERATE-DEMOCRAT	ULTRA-CONSERVATIVE
LIBERAL-DEMOCRAT	MODERATE-REPUBLICAN	RELIGIOUS RIGHT
	◄— LIBERTARIAN —►	CONSERVATIVE-REPUBLICAN
LEFT	MIDDLE	RIGHT

POLITICAL PARTY PLATFORMS

DEMOCRATIC PARTY PLATFORM

Democrats believe in reliance on government to solve all people's needs with an emphasis on taxation (in part to fund more bureaucracy). Democrats have an increased comfort level with larger government (especially at the federal level), and a belief in increased social programs, entitlements, and unionism. Democrats focus on those in lower economic society and have given these groups identities, such as "the poor and disadvantaged." They have a mistrust of the rich, large corporations, and business. Democrats are softer on crime and usually maintain smaller defense budgets. They believe strongly in pro-choice rights for abortion. Religion is not mainstream to their platform; they prefer to keep religion separate from government and politics. Democrats place strong emphasis on environmental concerns, and they align with more government involvement and socialist agendas, than with free-market principles.

The more liberal Democrat adheres to stronger beliefs in political correctness, heavy support of labor unions, and are adamant against religion in education, government, and politics. They are against individuals owning guns, they are for legalized same-sex marriage, and strong support for environmentalism, non-interventionalist foreign policy, globalism, and rights for illegal aliens. Liberals expect to accomplish these goals through tax payer dollars.

The roots of the Democrat Party can be traced back to the 1790s with Thomas Jefferson and James Madison. Established in 1848, the Democratic National Committee (DNC) oversees the Democrat Party. The DNC is responsible for overseeing and promoting the Democrat Party, formulating party platform, fundraising, and supporting candidates and Democrat campaigns and election strategy. Every four years the DNC oversees the National Convention. The DNC does not allow dissenting opinions on such issues as abortion and gay marriage at their national conventions. The National Education Association, one of the largest educator organizations, usually has the most delegates to the Democratic National Convention.

Democrats promote themselves as helping persons of low income, but do so through income redistribution, via federal government, by increasing taxes on all other citizens. The Democrat Party, because of its platform has been referred to as: 1) *The Party of the People;* 2) *The Tax and Spend Party;* 3) *The Party of Change, or Progressive Party;* 3) *Gloom and Doom Party.*

REPUBLICAN PARTY PLATFORM

Republicans and conservatives believe that government should be limited; government should be utilized only to keep order and protection, with limited taxation, but a strong military defense.

They believe in the power, self reliance, independence, and personal responsibility of the individual. Republicans believe in free-market enterprise, capitalism, and entrepreneurship. They believe in preservation of social and cultural values, traditions, religion, morality, and in pro-life, not the abortion of a fetus. They believe that individuals can make the best decisions, not government.

The Republican Party was founded in the early 1850s with its first official meeting in July 1854 in Jackson, Michigan, where its platform was established and candidates were nominated. The party was created to address the issues of anti-slavery (abolitionist movement), and the belief that the government should grant western lands free to settlers. Its birthplace is considered to be Ripon, Wisconsin where its earliest activists first gathered. Its name came from Thomas Jefferson's Democratic-Republican Party (this later became the Democratic Party).

At this time in our nation's history the Republican Party was a third party going against the nationally established Democratic and Whig Parties. In 1856 the new party reached national recognition when its first nominated candidate for president, John C. Fremont, won 33 percent of the vote. Then, in 1860, Abraham Lincoln became the first Republican president. Because the southern economy relied so heavily on slavery, slavery was a major issue that helped ignite the Civil War. Against the advice of his cabinet, Lincoln signed the Emancipation Proclamation during the war. This document freed all slaves. Republicans were instrumental in enacting additional legislation to outlaw slavery, give equal protection under the laws, and voting rights for African-Americans. The first woman elected to Congress, Jeanette Rankin in 1917, was a Republican from Montana.

The Republican National Committee (RNC) oversees the Republican Party. It provides national leadership for the party by developing and promoting its platform, fund raising, election strategy, and overseeing the Republican National Convention. The Republican Party platform is referred to as: 1) *The Grand Old Party (GOP)*; 2) *The Voice of Reason.*

MIDDLE PARTY PLATFORM

The Middle Party believes in maintaining a central position as opposed to two predominant polarized choices. They believe in mediation of policies and issues, and may polarize on some issues more than others. They are a melting of opposing ideologies that address the majority population. A middle party is true democracy by the majority of the citizen population; it maintains a centrist view of society and culture.

Independent parties have traditionally sprung up during times of political turmoil where the populous is divided on issues or concerns. This is how the Republican Party got its start, over the slavery issue. But few independent or middle parties have longevity after the issue has passed. This has remained a characteristic of third parties since the national two-party system developed. There are independent parties that are based on national coverage but are not able to carry a national election. It is a firm belief that America would be a stronger nation if the populous would accept a strong national Independent Party. It would give more choice of candidates and act as a balance to the other parties.

Many other nations function with multiple parties. The National Tea Party movement that developed just after the 2008 presidential campaign was an independent movement back to our founding principles. The Middle Party has been referred to as: 1) *The Independent Party*; 2) *The Third Party*; 3) *The Centrist Party.*

HOW PERSONALTY STYLES DETERMINE POLITICS

It is interesting to see Personality Styles projected across a political platform. There is liberal thought at one end, and conservative thought at the other, but the majority, hover in the middle. It is my belief that the Supporter and Analytic Personality Styles are the ones who determine political elections, whether polarized to the left or right. What I mean by this is, even though the Supporter is aligned with the Promoter with their emphasis on the well-being of people, the Supporter will hover back and forth across center based on individual characteristics and personality of the politician running for office. The Analytic likes order and is also sympathetic to people in that they do not want conflict, but for everyone to get along. The Analytic is a good observer. In this respect, their political views mirror the characteristics of their Personality Style, and, therefore, they have a tendency to hover back and forth over the center of political issues.

Analytics and Supporters are influenced more by personality and environment than platform. They vote more based on the individual candidate and concerns of the day. At other times, they are swayed by a single issue. A good example would be educators who vote for Democrat candidates in hopes of more school funding. Another is union workers who vote Democrat because of favoritism of the Democrat Party to unions. Others vote strongly conservative because of concerns about taxation, business, and the political effects on free market issues, and belief in limiting government growth and influence. Those concerned about issues related to defense, community safety, and crime, tend to also vote more conservative. Director Personality Styles generally vote conservative whereas Promoters vote predominantly liberal.

Analytics and Supporters are naturally polarized either left or right in their ideology. In addition to this natural political instinct, other factors are the environment in which they were raised, and the political conscience of the era, all helping to formulate their political view. When one is influenced and accepts the values of one's parents it is termed *political socialization*.

With the Promoter Personality being strongly liberal, and the Director Personality strongly conservative, it is the Supporter and Analytic that tip elections to one side or the other. In all social and political interactions, as you take issues out to the edges, people begin to disagree.

The Political Bell Chart illustrates this.

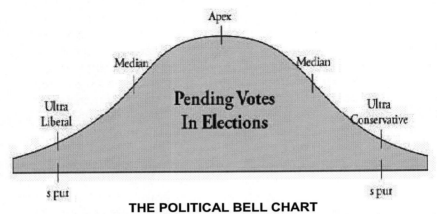

THE POLITICAL BELL CHART

As you go farther out to the extreme on the Political Bell Chart, behaviors become non-negotiable. That is to say, as you move out to the foot of the bell chart the political belief is cemented. Those persons will not read a book about or look into opposing political views to change or moderate their political views.

LIBERALISM
DEMOCRATIC PARTY
Reliance on govt. /Socialism

MODERATE MIDDLE
INDEPENDENT PARTY
Center / Middle of road

CONSERVATIVISM
REPUBLICAN PARTY
Limited govt. /Capitalism

MYOPIC LENS OF SOCIETY

With optical industry experience in the author's background, another way to look at this is optically. There are two main types of lens correction in eyeglasses, one is for farsightedness and is corrected by plus (+) lenses, which are thicker in the center and magnify objects. The opposite style lens minus (-), is for correction of nearsightedness, and is shaped as a concave lens to bend light. In either case, both lenses must be fit optically over a person's pupil or distortion will occur in the form of prism effect. Prism bends light rays, and can, especially in high power prescriptions, be an optician's nightmare by distorting vision.

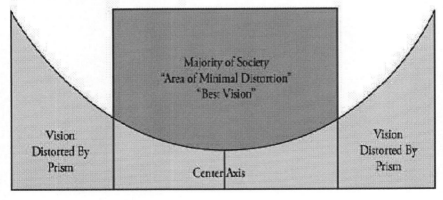

IDEOLOGY AND DEFINITION FROM OUR YOUTH

A LIBERAL. I have heard the following comments from our young describing what they believe a liberal to be.

- Federal government is here to serve the people, and needs the power to do so. Government can than institute social programs through redistribution and progressive taxation to help the poor, single mothers, the elderly, the oppressed, and other unfortunate groups.

- Liberalism is a mature way to embrace individual differences, not with ancient religious dogma or prejudice.

- Liberals are outspoken about other's rights and perceived oppression, and question authority. Free thinkers, they don't rely on tradition and antiquated religious dogma to live their lives and formulate their views.

- They support atheists, gays, African-Americans, pro-choice, and intellectuals.

- Liberals want less restriction on abortion, gender and race equality, free choice in sexual orientation, and separation of church and state, but more restrictions on guns and military budgets.

- Liberals are responsible for the emancipation and suffrage of blacks, teaching evolution, and other social changes considered controversial by conservatives. Fundamentalists see this as immoral but is the progressive way to deal with social differences.

- Liberals protect the environment.

- Liberals believe in the rights of people over corporations, and weaken corporations with higher taxation, environmental regulations, and support of unions.

- Liberals also believe in more taxation for the wealthy, while reducing taxes for the poor.

- Liberals do not support multinational corporations because of lack of control and regulation over them, and feel they take advantage of developing countries and exploit child labor.

- Liberals prefer nationalization (socialization) of industry so wealth and power is not concentrated with just a few, but with the people. Liberals use diplomacy instead of war.

It is interesting to read all the positive statements given the liberal, but the ultimate means in which to accomplish these things is what is at question, and not a consideration in the above. Liberal solutions are always an infringement upon others, especially those that have worked hard to get ahead. With decades of liberal influence and dogma, liberals have the United States in their tentacles.

In the above descriptions, you can see the belief in strong federal government utilized for social programs, a basic ideology of the Democrat platform, and their paternal obsession with "unfortunate groups" (the poor, the elderly, the uneducated, the oppressed, etc.). It also only credits liberals for social programs, then refers to liberalism as "a mature way to embrace individual differences not with ancient religious dogma or prejudice." This is a blatant attack on tradition, social justice, and moral values. It degrades the culture already put in place by core American values, with no acknowledgement of the many deaths of patriots over a 200 year history to keep us free.

In the above we also see an emphasis of the liberal's belief in larger government and overseeing the free market. In recent years liberal administrations have interceded into the free market. A minimal military budget, funding education, improving wages and social programs, and protecting the environment, on the surface all seem admirable. But it is the degree, and the dollar amount, and the way of funding such issues, that is always in question along with the usual lack of foresight that causes problems for the future (for example, the housing collapse).

It is also ironic that the liberal has been credited with the freedom and suffrage of blacks in America, when it was the first Republican, Abraham Lincoln, who fought for, and signed into law the Emancipation Proclamation document during the American Civil War. This monumental proclamation ultimately gave freedom to all slaves. This legislation was followed by several Constitutional amendments guaranteeing the rights of all citizens to vote regardless of their race. It was not until the 1960s, with civil rights demonstrations and equal rights legislation, that Southern Democrats were forced to treat blacks equally. Liberals would like to take credit for freeing the slaves, but it was Republicans who did it. Many people do not realize that Martin Luther King was a Republican.

Also, in the above comments there lacks an acknowledgement that people and politicians from all spectrums wish to help those truly in need. Overall, those on the left have too much trust of government.

Misunderstanding of free market condition, and too much overt trust in big government has always been a slippery slope for those on the left. Too much regulation or oversight of the free market causes economic downturns. The young liberal commentators seem totally oblivious to how a free society functions and how a free market economy works. Economy is essential for any political system's survival, regardless of the type of government. In all political systems there must be a means of supply and demand.

On the other hand, conservatives have been painted as the cause of America's woes and have been the left's scapegoat. This is what decades of liberal undermining have created. This is the way our American youth have been indoctrinated by the left. The following are comments by young people describing their understanding of what they believe it means to be a Republican. These beliefs are based on what has been taught to our youth by our education system, current culture, and the media. Look at the attitude toward Republicans and conservatives that have been instilled in our youth with decades of ever-expansive liberal ideology.

A REPUBLICAN. I have heard the following comments from the young describing what they believe a Republican to be.

- Someone who thinks it is okay to govern a nation based on a religion; a rich person trying to better themself.
- Republicans are heartless and selfish, intolerant racists.
- A Republican tries to sway the masses with use of patriotism and does not hesitate to send adults into war, but is opposed to taking a non-thinking embryo from a teenager.
- Republicans like giving tax cuts to the rich but do not like giving welfare to the poor.
- Republicans are always whining about how Democrats control the media but the media is owned by rich Republicans.
- They are white male Christians.
- Republicans also put guns in the hands of the wrong people.
- Republicans abuse their power through deregulation and lobbyists.
- They try to keep us fearful by use of terrorism and hide behind Christianity.
- They are rich and greedy, motivated only by money, and they do not care about the environment, but exploit it for their own gain.

It is sad what the liberal left has done to the minds of our young. How they espouse themselves as the sensitive overseers of the world to mask their insecurities, and their lust for power. It is criminal how they position themselves while always having a deeper agenda. This is not healthy for a nation or any political entity. It only serves to undermine and fracture the core of that nation.

You can see the liberal insecurities in the propaganda that has been consistently presented to our youth. For example, the ways in which Republicans have been demonized as a "hated group." Describing a Republican as "an intolerant racist person", and that they do not hesitate to send adults to war, but do not believe in abortion for a teenager. It is also interesting the reference that Republicans are, "white male Christians." All this has been indoctrinated by the liberal left. What is disconcerting is the depth of indoctrination that has been done to our youth, from a political platform stating that they are for the people (See, "Liberal Myths" in Chapter Three).

Over forty years of unchallenged liberalism has swept across our great nation promoting its ideology. It is sad how those of leftist political dogma have exploited our young, our society, our values and ethics, discrediting anything conservative. Just the fact they have done this is proof and caution enough to how credible such a liberalist ideology is. Ironically, it relies heavily on monetary support from the same portion of the society it condemns. For decades, because of good economy and world stability we saw these liberal ideological changes steadily become dictates in our society. We would complain and make comments how liberalized our schools were becoming as a topic of conversation, and how politically correct everything was becoming. How illegal aliens were receiving full citizenship rights, and how our increased taxes were paying for all this, and how sensitivity training was mandated. All these things happened around us, and even though we did not agree with it we let it happen. All these were passed into law before our eyes and we did not react because things were going well for us. Jobs were available for dual income families, disposable income could purchase a recreational vehicle or second home, our children could go to college. Our basic needs were being met, and we were busy living.

However, the scenario changed drastically within the first decade of the new millennium. We were reminded that we still had enemies of our freedom and democracy with the occurrence of 9/11. Our nation was launched into a two-front war with our children being sent to active combat zones in countries with a culture we knew little about, and who did not approve of our ways or our religion. Then the housing market toppled and brought many industries down with it. The economy changed almost immediately for most Americans. Jobs became scarce, and the market took a dive. During this same crisis a new president was elected who was to be the culmination of the liberal overtaking of America.

But the economy is how presidents are judged, and President Obama, seizing the opportunity to consummate the gains of the liberal left, added large deficits (never before in history) to an already struggling economy, and began to cross the comfort zone of most Americans by heavily involving government into private industry, economy, and into personal life with socialized healthcare. These were overt actions to the socialist culmination of how our society had been infiltrated for the last four decades. It took this economic realization and an overtly leftist president to make Americans take a stand. Easily within another decade, these growing liberal indoctrinations would be almost impossible to reverse, and in essence would implode in upon itself (See, "The 2008 Campaign", "Too Much Sensitivity & The Housing Collapse", and "The Day America Stood Still" in the Appendix).

What the liberal left does not want the populous to know is that Republicans and conservatives believe in family values, are good parents, upstanding citizens, are responsible members of the community, and are motivated employees and entrepreneurs. They are proud of the United States of America and its history and heritage. These beliefs and actions are the key to a strong base for raising future generations with good traits to be good citizens.

CHAPTER TWO

LIBERAL VERSES CONSERVATIVE

A man younger than thirty who's not a liberal has no heart, and a man older than thirty who's not a conservative has no brain.
~ Winston Churchill

Government is not reason, it is not eloquence, it is force; like fire, a troublesome servant and a fearful master. Never for a moment should it be left to irresponsible action. *~ George Washington*

The following table compares ideologies between the two political poles. It puts in perspective the basis of polarized social and political beliefs.

LIBERAL VIEW	CONSERVATIVE VIEW
A purist attitude toward mankind, when mankind fails it is because luck is against him and opportunity did not go his way. If successful, liberals believe that luck just came your way.	Realist in their attitude toward the world, mankind and life. It is accepted that mankind does have flaws that have been prevalent throughout history and it is not just hope & luck that makes a person successful, it is mostly hard work & individual effort.
Everyone should have free choice in every facet of their life; government should be there to supply your every need. Liberals want maximum social freedom supported by government.	Conservatives believe in the power of the individual and that government should be at arm's length, not dominating their existence. Individuals should be free to make choices and not be hampered by overt government.
Liberals overlook and do not acknowledge the shortcomings of human nature.	Conservatives accept the inconsistency of the human being and make allowances for it (i.e. rules & structure).
Liberals view the world through feelings and emotions, less on fact or detail.	Conservatives prefer reality & substantive proof, details, logic, data, balance sheets, etc.
Liberals believe that government made America.	Conservatives know the individual is the backbone of America & personal freedom built America. Individual effort keeps us strong and free.
Liberals believe the average person is too naïve and not responsible enough to be trusted to help themselves, and therefore need the help of government to make decisions & solutions for them.	Individuals are capable of their own destiny; it is individual initiative that has created everything that we have in America. Individual choice creates democratic government.
Liberals believe in the concept of group identity not individual identity.	Conservatives consider people as individuals, and respect individual rights, as written in the Constitution.
Liberals believe in total choice, not to be restricted by tradition or religious dogma. They believe in change over that of tradition, cultural & moral norms. Liberals do not hesitate to challenge established social norms and traditions.	Conservatives believe in protecting and preserving time-honored traditions and morals. They believe in change, but gradual change with proper preparation, with risks considered.
Liberals believe in definite separation of church and state.	Conservatives believe that without religion, politicians and government easily becomes tyrannical.

Politically, Promoters have a natural mistrust of conservatives, and feel that anything on the right to be quelling, restrictive, and generally suspicious. As their individual Promoter Personality Style reveals, they have a natural envy and suspicion of those who do better, especially in economic standards. Even though the Promoter Personality perceives the conservative right as insensitive, self-centered and greedy, at the same time they do not rationalize how their own Personality Style characteristics are perceived by the populace. Equating these characteristics politically, the Promoter's never-ending search for excitement, fun, freedom, attention, self-gratification, emotion, and security, compounded with lack of details in their personal life and political platform, is, at the least, unnerving to the average voter.

As you know, the Promoter craves attention and draws their energy from others. As a national platform, the Promoter's focus is emotional sensitivity to groups they feel are in need. The extreme of this has been described as being a "bleeding heart liberal". But this same sensitivity also puts them in a dilemma which affects their good judgment, and usually the reality of the situation. For example, those on the left never seem to know when enough is enough in helping a group. As what will be discussed later is that Promoters, those on the left in the political context, quizzically always put people in "groups" not as individuals. Promoters over-sensitize everything and every issue, and at times even appear irrational. If you project the characteristics of the Promoter Personality Style to a national political platform, you have the Democrat Party.

Even though liberalism and the concept of the Nanny State were pre-empted by the Woodrow Wilson (1913) and the FDR administrations (1930), the spark of liberalism was reignited in the 1960s. It nurtured and grew roots through the 1970s, and when the older generation at the time grew out of their influence on society through attrition, liberalism blossomed throughout the1980s and came to full bloom in the 1990s, from which it is still dominant. There have been conservative presidents to buffer the slide to the left, but society still continued its slide influenced by the ongoing indoctrination from the left.

In the 1970s, judges were swept by the ever growing liberal society to the point where prison sentences were reduced. Murder was fifteen years or less with good behavior. This changed with public outcry and refocus of societal concern. This was one portion of society that had to take a step back from the growing liberalism, while other aspects of the judicial system continued to move to the left, such as prisoner's rights, and environment concerns, rights for illegal aliens, as well as sexual orientation.

The Promoter Personality tends to worry a lot; they are born more emotional about their world around them. Emotional people worry more about things and are paranoid about power and influence when it is not in their control. They are most comfortable about their world and their existence when they have the power. This is especially true with political power and having government at their whim. Therefore, the Democrat Party has been referred to as the, *Gloom and Doom Party*, since it attaches much emotion to its worried agenda. With the liberal side of the political spectrum, more policies and proposals are made out of emotion than from the baseline of a budget or balance sheet. Again, Promoters do not like to have a lot of details or data. Those on the left can generally woo the masses, whereas conservatives are more structured, independent, business-like and more matter-of-fact, which tends to pass them off to the general public as benign and less caring.

Even when a political liberal does an unethical or unpopular act, or an injustice while in office (such as former President Clinton with Monica Lewinsky), liberal constituents do not jump ship, but ride it down into the depths with their candidate. This resolve is also true of conservatives, but morals have a much stronger influence with conservatives. Clinton's act, behavior, and self-indulgent arrogance should have been dealt with severely, so future presidents establish upstanding morals in the office of the President. Evidently, liberals were caught in their customary emotion and were in denial and did not consider the future aspect of such an act and behavior. In addition to this, since the incident occurred, there has been very little public remorse on the part of Mr. Clinton, which fits in directly with the Promoter psyche of self-absorption, perceived by others as arrogance; not being wrong (he lied directly to the camera when questioned about the facts pertaining to Ms. Lewinsky), dislike of rules, and the propensity for manipulative behavior. These are classic Promoter Personality Style traits. And remember, Promoter Personalities are at their best during crises.

This same liberal scenario is played out with President Barack Obama. Liberals were vocalizing and criticizing the Bush Administration for a federal budget deficit of $800 billion. But in only a few short months under the Obama Administration the budget deficit had reached over a trillion dollars[1], however those same critical voices remained quiet.

This shows the height of liberal hypocrisy. Unfortunately, they chose party over country.

When a local or national disaster occurs, emotion takes over the left side of the political spectrum and they want to change everything right then and there while the hype and emotion remains. There is little regard to budget and resources. An easy solution, of course, is to raise taxes. Therefore, liberals are criticized as being short on plans in their politics. On the other hand, conservatives approach tragedies and disasters from a more fiscal perspective. They maintain a larger national defense budget for such emergencies, and utilize more of a managed approach to such tragedies. The memory and record widespread destruction of hurricane Katrina should reinforce to both Republicans and Democrats, that a nation should always be prepared.

It is difficult to break the hold of liberalism once it has been nurtured and grown over the course of time. You might say that liberalism began in California in the *Haight-Ashbury district* (where the Hippie Movement supposedly began), and continued through the United States, across to Europe, South Africa, to Asia and so on. The only area of the world with limited liberal change is that of the Muslim world.

As with anything personal or political, too much of anything has its downside. In the case of liberalism, it creates an ultimate erosion of individual responsibility and individualistic pioneer spirit, the two things that made this country what it is. And unfortunately, liberals can never have enough liberalism. The demarcation between liberalism and socialism is vague.

A liberal society, if left unchecked by a periodic balance of conservative elected candidates, would implode in upon itself because social gifting would remain unchecked. Entitlements and social programs would swell the budget and bureaucracy. There would be a miniscule budget remaining for military defense. Taxation would be a cure-all to support the ever increasing social programs while the cost of living would soar. There would be fewer rich, less businesses and entrepreneurship -- why start a business when the government overwhelmingly taxes you on your hard work and initiative? This is what caused the Great Depression to continue for so long. President Franklin Roosevelt refused to reduce taxes on small businesses and entrepreneurs, and raised taxes five times between 1933 and 1939 to pay for the ever increasing government. World War II is what stopped the Great Depression not FDR (See, "The Day America Stood Still" in the Appendix).

At this state, society would quickly reach a '
in economy and family income. It would be
emphasis on government. We as a culture ar
our entrepreneurial spirit, and our individual
been eroded because of unrealistic expect
has been said, that with a liberal society, "T
way when right is wrong, and wrong is right.

In retrospect, in a conservative-driven society, responsibility is μ..
on the individual. Even John F. Kennedy, as a Democrat, must have
understood the potential devastation of on-going liberalism and the
creation of large government when JFK[2] himself penned into his
inauguration speech, "Ask not what your country can do for you; ask
what you can do for your country." This was during the age of moderate
fiscally responsible Democrats.

The conservative is the liberal's scapegoat, those on the left always
paint conservatives as arrogant, self-absorbed, anti-social, greedy
hypocrites. Knowing its hypocrisy and inconsistencies, it is surprising
to see the affinity that people have for the Democrat Party. The public
accepts and buys into the Promoters' smoke screen. In reality, the
conservative has a good heart, is patriotic, and is for social justice,
but also for personal responsibility. Conservatives are down-to-earth
and are for a free market economy. For these reasons the Republican
Party at times has been referred to as the "Grand Old Party."

Just as we hear Islamic extremists say all their problems are derived
from Israel, likewise you hear liberals say all their problems are derived
from conservatives. A similar edict is heard from conservatives. This
does not make sense, since in reality the parties should balance each
other. The only way these two factions will work efficiently together
is if they have competition from the middle. By playing the blame
game, both parties do an injustice to their constituents. Nothing gets
done. This explains one of the reasons the American public is very
disappointed with Congress and consistently gives it a low rating.

THE DICHOTOMY OF THE FAR LEFT PYSCHE
Take a Promoter Personality who does not like rules, dwells on the
abstract in life, has an overt ego with limited religious affiliation and
you have a liberal. Liberals want to win. They want to be on top. Their
only redeeming characteristic is they are very emotional and overly
sensitive, which creates a concern for others, but this is secondary
to their needs. This sensitivity has a price and it comes full circle with

. Given the inherent characteristics of the Promoter there
n offsetting analytic anchor. Sooner or later liberals shoot
s in the foot, and therefore, could not exist indefinitely without
etting of fiscal responsibility (as we learned, the Promoter and
tic complement each other).

hose on the left are dichotomous, they want free choice in their
life, but rely heavily on government and its overt directives. Again,
we see the Promoter Personality at play because it must seek its
organization and structure from an outside source, i.e. the Analytic (or
on a national basis, the structure of government). Therefore, millions
of Promoters, elevated to a national party, cling onto government for
their structure and security. Big government gives liberals a feeling of
security and power.

Based on the psyche and political platform of the Democratic Party,
there should be no rich liberals (or Democrats), but if you look at a cross-
section of the Democrats in Congress, there are many millionaires. It
is another dichotomy why they don't turn most of their money over to
the poor like they want everyone else to do via taxes. One could only
assume that wealthy liberals and Democrats are hypocritical (See,
"Predominant Liberal Myths" in Chapter Three, "Myth 1: The Rich Do
Not Pay Enough Taxes").

The mere fact that liberals get rich on our system, the system they
say they hate so much and want to change or destroy, is hypocrisy.
These same liberals would not exist comfortably, or for very long, in a
true socialist or communist system because they could not enjoy the
same quality of life or opportunities a free market system gives. They
would miss the freedoms our system offers, both our constitutional
rights and free market enterprise. These hypocrisies reinforce the lack
of foresight and inability to draw a line, or to say no, with a psyche
based only on the utopian dream of total equality. It has been said that,
"Liberals always ride on the titter-tatter of hypocrisy."

Pro-choice and the debate over when life begins is another dichotomy
of the liberal world. They will protect the environment, even at the
detriment of the citizenry and the poor (for example, not drilling in
environmental areas even when energy prices are at all time highs).
They protect the environment and worry about pollution and global
warming, but the hypocrisy is that they are less apt to worry about
the unborn. During the McCain-Obama campaign with gasoline prices
increasing, the Democrat campaign was steadfast when their own

countrymen were threatened by economic loss because of increasing energy prices created by their reluctance to allow drilling within our environmental sphere. Even though they did not have a specific short term energy plan, they refused to consider opening up environmental areas for safe exploration. With our technology, drilling can be safe and the environment protected (As the reader moves through this writing, other dichotomies and hypocrisies of the left will be obvious. See, "Predominant Liberal Myths" in Chapter Three, "Myth 3: The Natural Resources Are All Being Destroyed, And Global Warming Is Going To Destroy The Earth").

Along with the belief the Promoter has of the faultlessness of mankind, there is a natural bias against religious ideology, since it acknowledges the weakness and sinful nature of mankind. This is more hypocrisy of the liberal psyche. The left condones and mistrusts those that are religious, especially the Religious Right. One cannot understand why this is; except that it must present a moral structuring that liberals dislike. Remember, the Promoter wants freedom and empowerment and no restraints.

Another intriguing hypocrisy is the support of unionism. A party platform that supports free choice when it comes to birth and abortion, you would think would also believe in free choice when it comes to the workplace and selecting a job. It would make sense if the party platform would be for independent contracting and free choices for the individual worker, but that is not the case since liberals mistrust business and large corporations and focus on group identity rather than on individuals. Cities such as New York are hog-tied by their unionism and lack of non-union competition. It is the unions that have made New York such an expensive place to live. In the same manner, the high cost of living in Massachusetts is caused from many generations of liberal political ideology. This is also prevalent in San Francisco and other large left-leaning cities throughout America.

Those on the left are also lenient on illegal immigration, and at the same time reduce our military, which puts the people of America in a double jeopardy regarding safety, especially since Islamic extremists have declared a religious war on the United States. Those on the left have an ambivalent view toward terrorism and patriotism, letting sensitivity override their common sense, and therefore, they see terrorists both as a menace, but also as an oppressed group.

The following illustrations show the difference between the cognitive psyche of conservatives and liberals.

Single Layer of the Conservative Psyche

Is the same all the way
To the Bottom

Only One Layer

To the Bottom

- *Decisions based on facts, data & logic with bottom line perspective*
- *Consideration and concern for future outcomes*
- *Belief in capitalism and free market system*
- *Belief in the individual and personal endeavor, tradition & religion*

In comparison to the conservative, in the following chart it is easy to see the multiple layers of the liberal psyche. From my observation, it is obvious that many Democrats remain only on the upper surface of this ideology their entire lives. I refer to these persons as *Surface Democrats*, since they do not delve any deeper into the Democrat psyche. A personal example of this is with a relative of mine. During her lifetime, she has only floated on the top level of the chart. Through the years, whenever a Democrat disgraced himself, or was unpopular because of their agenda or issues, my relative has consistently sunk to the depths with the candidate. This is detrimental to the health and safety of our society. There are times when we all need to step out of our party, to save the nation. The Democrats need to do this with Barack Obama. Overtly motivated by power and control those on the left struggle with this, because they never take the time to examine the deeper levels of psyche at play. This may also explain why there are Democrat incumbents that change from their Party to the Libertarian, or Republican Party, because they are at odds with the deeper ideology. They must have experienced the deeper level of the liberal psyche, and no longer wanted to be part of its ideology.

Multiple Layers of the Liberal Psyche

Most of the populous gets shrouded in *The Smoke Screen*	Some perceive but do not see through *The Murk*	Fewer perceive and really understand *The Liberals' True Nature*

Layer 1

The Smoke Screen (Rhetoric heard in conversation & elections)

- *Very influencing and promoting of their philosophy*
- *Likeable surface personality & say what you want to hear*
- *Espouse sensitivity & appear to hold humanity at the forefront*

Layer 2

Area of Transition (Clouded and mixed signals)

- *Populous gets duped into the liberals' sensitivity bias*

Deep Psyche of the Liberal   Layer 3

- *Very competitive, single-focused and self-promoting with limited foresight*
- *Excels in being in power which gives them ultimate security and few restrictions*
- *Do not believe people truly are capable of helping themselves without government oversight*
- *No compassion & condescending for those who have done well, or for the individual because everything is fit into a group dynamic*
- *Unaccepting about those that do not agree with them*
- *Suspicious of big business, corporations and those who have done well*
- *Feels restricted by tradition & religion*

DEALING WITH PERSONALITY STYLE ADVERSITY

It seems that envy, jealousy, and the lust for power are in the genes from the start with those on the left. This single focus, oversensitive, fiscal apathy, and unquenchable desire for power are dominant characteristics of their psyche. They created the hated class to describe those persons and entrepreneurs who have done better for themselves, and corporations that have been successful. This, liberals feel, gives them the right, via government, to mandate taxes on those who, through hard work and ambition, have done better.

What is astonishing is when these liberals are well off, based on their own ideological belief, you would think that they would be the first to give away their own personal wealth. Instead they keep wishing to take money from the hated class, which, by their own definition, they are now a participant. It is not normal, especially with any conscience, to select a "class" and then try to destroy that class. What liberals will not acknowledge is that those who have done better have done so through their own hard work, dedication, and good personal decisions. The hypocrisies are many among liberal ideology. It is because of these contradictions, that it is stressed in this writing, not to take those on the left seriously when in their hyper-state about a policy, issue, decision, or event. Wait them out; let their torch burn down first. Liberals tend to be two-edged swords, in any interactions with them, be aware of their deep-seated insecurities and need for power and control.

Adversity and conflict are difficult to avoid in interpersonal and political interaction. Whenever in a political or personal dispute, look at the core characteristics of the Personality Style of your opponent and offset those characteristics. For example, with the Promoter Personality, whenever discussing an issue, it is usually going to be approached with emotion and generally a lack of specific details. On issues, do not initially accept their position. Wait for the hype, emotion, pomp-and-circumstance to pass before you consider them viable. Remember, the Promoter also likes center stage and attention. Your best rebuttal is to have facts and details to nullify the emotional response. Bring them "back down to earth" with rational budget analyzed figures. You must first burst their emotional bubble as they are easiest discredited by facts, which they will deny (See, "How To Deal With A Liberal Opponent" in the Appendix).

THE INDIVIDUAL, ANOTHER DICHOTOMY FOR THE LEFT

The Constitution is based on individual rights, not group rights. Everything in the constitution is for the individual, guaranteeing individual rights. Although people on a one-to-one social basis are important to liberals, individual rights are cumbersome for their political platform. Individual rights tend to be a precarious hypocrisy for liberal ideology. Liberals do not think in terms of individuals, but as groups: *the poor, the unfortunate, the oppressed, the Hispanics, the Native Americans, etc.* By speaking in terms of groups, it blends better with the liberal view of big government and social entitlement intertwined. The liberal approach to the poor, for instance, is to consider them one class, "the poor", and "the less fortunate."

If those on the left were to dwell on individualistic rights, it would move them away from their security and ideological collectivism, which is big government. This is the view which also follows popular socialistic ideology. Remember, the United States Constitution gives rights only to the individual, not to any one group. It would be disastrous if the Constitution had given rights not only to the individual, but also to a few select groups. If this had been the case, our nation would be a totally different place, and resemble more the politics of the Middle East where one group, or ruler, takes over and does not allow any social or political diversity.

Based on this same psyche, the left does not consider the poor to be poor because of decisions they made personally. Such as their choice not to continue in high school, or go to college, or get a second job to better their condition, or the forethought to wait and have children once they are better prepared, or the decision to buy those adult toys before paying rent. Liberals fully believe "the poor" came into their condition because they were just unlucky. This is a big criticism from conservatives, that, "liberals always want to save us from ourselves." This is the same underlying insecurity Promoters have, and is why they like the security and deep pockets that government can give them. After all, if they do not have good luck, because of limited ambition, poor planning in life, and lack of discipline in saving, they still have government to take care of them.

To make a person an individual, functioning citizen, is not an easy task after four plus decades of liberal whitewash. You must first get them to believe in themselves again, and in their abilities. They must be weaned off entitlement programs and social gifting, and learn that big government is not a cure all, but comes with severe backlashes and mandates of every kind. Once they realize America is still a country of individuals, with individual rights for each of us, their confidence will build and they will become independent productive citizens.

The U.S. Constitution guarantees you individual freedom of speech, freedom of religion, the right to bear arms, etc. Don't ever take it for granted! Remember these rights and always hold them dear. Many individuals have lost their lives, and will continue to do so, to uphold our Constitution, whereby, guaranteeing us our individual freedoms from tyranny and our own government. Here is where the buck stops. If there were no Constitution, or if it had not been written for the individual, liberals would have government breathing down our neck in every capacity of our life. The liberal direction of this nation over several decades has challenged these individual freedoms and has moved us ever closer to socialism (See, "The Constitution" in the Appendix).

The following illustrates the socialist spiral we are on, with liberalism the precursor to greater restrictions of freedom.

CHAPTER THREE

PREDOMINANT LIBERAL MYTHS

It is error alone which needs the support of government. Truth can stand by itself.
                                                                    ~ Thomas Jefferson

A liberal's main goal is utopian equality. They want total freedom of choice, protection of the environment, and to extend social programs and entitlements to make us all equal. Liberals tend to protect us from ourselves. You will hear the following myths expressed by those on the left in their speeches and ideology, and in their political platforms directed against conservatives, and to those that do not follow their liberal psyche:

1) **The Rich Do Not Pay Enough Taxes**
2) **Large Corporations Are Evil And Control The World**
3) **The Natural Resources Are All Being Destroyed, And Global Warming Is Going To Destroy The Earth**
4) **We Never Spend Enough On Education**
5) **Government Is The Answer To Everything, It Should Take Care Of All Things**
6) **Republicans And Conservatives Are Cold, Insensitive People, Who Only Want To Become Rich**

Myth 1: The Rich Do Not Pay Enough Taxes

As we have learned, there is an inherent mistrust, fear, and jealousy by liberals toward those individuals of good monetary means. Since the left is more socialist in their thought, liberals mistrust capitalism, large corporations, and those who have wealth, even though many prominent liberals and Democrats are well-to-do.

Promoter Personalities are competitive by nature. This is one reason why their belief in the myth that the rich do not pay enough taxes lives on in liberal circles. They are envious and suspicious of those who have done well for themselves and think of persons with wealth as only having been lucky and received breaks in life. Liberals seem to have a difficult time understanding the hard work and dedication that people with better means have put in to build companies that supply jobs to others.

The sad situation is that the liberal does not understand that these persons obtained their wealth through hard work. Instead, the liberal wants to build government bigger and bigger on these people's resources through taxation. They do not admit, nor give credit to entrepreneurs. The liberal easily forgets that companies pay the greatest portion of taxes and also employ their constituents who are also taxed on their work and personal efforts. Since the administration of President Eisenhower, the government has had to rely on 45 percent of its revenue from individual income taxes.

Based on year 2006, the top ten percent of the nation's tax payers with incomes of $108,904 or more, pay 71 percent of the taxes in this country. And these are the persons the left always wants to raise taxes on. Every large company was once a small company started by one or more individuals. Because of the opportunities still available in America, the middle class has continued to grow. The following IRS data reveals this disparity of who pays taxes, and how it has changed just within two years.

Percentage	Year 2004 taxes	Percent of incomes	Year 2006 taxes	Percent of incomes
Top 1%	pay 37% of taxes	19% over $328k	pay 40% of taxes	23% over $389k
Top 5%	pay 57% of taxes	33% over $137k	pay 60% of taxes	21% over $154k
Top 10%	pay 68% of taxes	44% over $99k	pay 71% of taxes	19% over $109k
Top 25%	pay 85% of taxes	66% over $60k	pay 86% of taxes	16% over $66k
Top 50%	pay 97% of taxes	87% over $30k	pay 97% of taxes	14% over $32k
Bottom 50%	pay only 3% of taxes	3% under $30k	pay only 3% of taxes	3% under $32k

Source: www.taxfoundation.org and www.irs.gov/taxstats.

These are issues magnified by the Promoter Personality. It is all perception. Just because conservatives deal a lot with business and free market commerce (the route to independence), many people, especially liberals, do not trust conservatives. Things do happen in large corporations and business, which liberals are quick to point out, such as Exxon and the more recent Madoff scandal. But those incidents are still rare compared to how companies are pilfered by their own employees and the taxes they have to pay to the government, all while they supply an income for many people. The amount of daily pilfering at companies, whether it is letterhead, pens, or embezzled funds, is an overwhelming amount when compared with the incidences periodically heard on the news about companies doing an injustice.

Psychologically, another reason why those whose ideologies hover on the left are consumed by what they call the "evils of corporations" is because they have little control over corporations, and therefore, feel insecure toward them. Those on the left in essence want total control in every aspect and become uncomfortable and suspicious when they do not. Bottom line, liberals want unlimited power socially and politically. This same attitude by the British to the early American colonies ultimately caused the cry, "Taxation without representation is tyranny" and the events that followed ultimately made us a free people.

The leftist message that the rich are dishonest and selfish, and came by their wealth in devious ways, has been instilled in generation after generation. It is now an unfounded cultural stereotype that is inbred in our society. It is not fair to those who have worked hard, taken the time and effort to get a good education, and therefore, good jobs, to be branded by those who have not made wise decisions, did not prepare, or do not have a good work ethic, or attitude. Such persons will naturally be envious of those that have done well for themselves. Outside of winning a lottery, those that have done well have done so through hard work, education, wise choices, and a willingness to take some risk, as summarized by the phrase, "no guts, no glory." It is easy for the Democrat left to exploit this stereotype; but no one can negate the reality that hard work and wise choices equals success. Poverty is caused by poor choices, irresponsibility, and lack of ambition.

The old adage, "the rich get richer and the poor get poorer," is partially true. As a generous society, we are ready to give those that have not done as well, our charity. Let's examine why the rich do better and the poor do not do as well. The rich keep themselves informed, they continue to educate themselves and make contacts, and continue to ambitiously pursue their goals. In short, they prepare for success. They keep abreast on events, trends, invest their money wisely, and take some risks. All this pays off and spells ultimate success. Like everyone else, the rich also have setbacks, but they keep forging on. If you leave the aforementioned things out of the equation, you have the reasons why the poor remain poor, or do not do as well as those who are better off.

In America everyone can still make a go of it. The potential is in each of us. Everyone can ultimately be successful and live comfortably, they just have to invest in themselves. Attesting to America still being the land of opportunity is that over half of those poor in this nation, are no longer poor ten years later. It must again be stressed that it is individual initiative and ambition that will make your dreams come true. The middle class of today live the lifestyle of the upper class of the 1950s; that is, with disposable income, multiple family vehicles, vacation travel, a family cabin, boat, and college education.

Business needs to make profit, or the government does not get paid. Capitalist competition lowers prices, but when the government manages a program there is no competition. If the plan does not work, taxes must be used instead to maintain the program, or makeup losses. Business and corporations are held to a higher scrutiny than government. Can you imagine, what the media would have done with the Monica Lewinski case had it occurred in a large corporation with a corporate executive playing the part of the president? There would be public disgust over the situation and the liberal side of the world would tell you, "I told you so; those large corporations need to be controlled more and taxed more so these atrocities do not occur." This is another double standard. The government has its own dark side to deal with, as does any government program, organization, or school district. There are plenty of abuses, poor management, arrogance, and inappropriate acts in each level of government. School districts alone periodically share the limelight on the six o'clock news with some of the incidences which have occurred in them.

Government spending does not rejuvenate the economy, and taxation quells production and incentive. It is speculative how long the top ten percent can continue to pay seventy one percent of the nation's taxes before they go out of business, into personal ruin, move out of state, or the country. The class that is grossly discriminated against and jeopardized by the liberal political sphere (the so called People's Party), is the same tax class that is keeping everything going (the top ten percent). With the legislation enacted during the writing of this book, the number of non-tax paying households has continued to increase.

I have asked those on the left, "Why do Democrats always have to raise taxes even in good economic times?" I have yet to receive an answer. Former President Bill Clinton was fortunate to be president in a politically non-challenging time, with a good economy, and therefore, should not have had to raise taxes, but he did. (See, "A Brief History of Federal Taxes" in the Appendix).

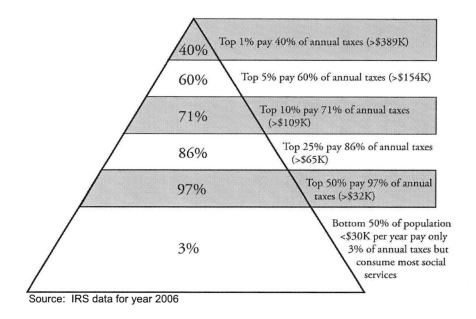

Source: IRS data for year 2006

The Unequal Tax Pyramid

As you see from the chart, the top 50 percent pay 97 percent of annual federal taxes. Therefore, government truly takes from individuals and redistributes to the lower 50 percent of the population. Government does not generate revenue through marketing and selling of a product, like entrepreneurs and businesses must, but by taxing individuals and businesses.

The most important thing to remember as a tax paying citizen is that since the pre-collection of taxes was never rescinded after World War Two, and probably never will be, the government has greatly reduced the tax payers awareness of the amount of taxes actually being collected, and how much less your paycheck is. The government made the payment of taxes less obvious and therefore much easier to raise taxes on the populous in the future.

Imagine what you could do with more disposable income throughout the year. The investment potential you would have and the ability to better control a family budget. The government has removed these freedoms from you by taking taxes out of your paycheck before you get it. Remember what Thomas Jefferson said, "A government big enough to give you everything you want, is strong enough to take everything you have."

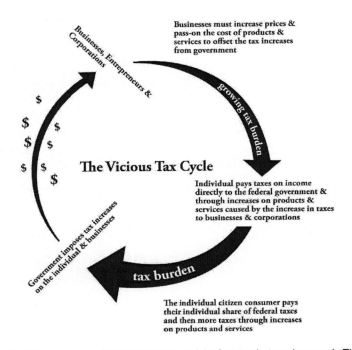

The Vicious Tax Cycle

Businesses, Entrepreneurs & Corporations

Businesses must increase prices & pass-on the cost of products & services to offset the tax increases from government

growing tax burden

Individual pays taxes on income directly to the federal government & through increases on products & services caused by the increase in taxes to businesses & corporations

tax burden

Government imposes tax increases on the individual & businesses

The individual citizen consumer pays their individual share of federal taxes and then more taxes through increases on products and services

The fine line between government, taxpayers, and the free market can be seen in The Vicious Tax Cycle. The relationship government and the free market have is akin to the separation of church and state. They are separate entities, but affect each other. Taxes imposed by the government can adversely affect the free market system and the individual tax paying consumer. The individual is the basic unit of the economy. All tax increases directly and indirectly fall on the individual, including increased taxes on businesses and corporations which are passed onto the individual consumer.

Tax comparison between Presidents Clinton and George W. Bush

Taxes under Clinton 1999
Single @ 30K income tax $8,400
Single @ 50K income tax $14,000
Single @ 75K income tax $23,250
Married @ 60K income tax $16,800
Married @ 75K income tax $21,000
Married @ 125K income tax $38,750

Taxes under Bush 2008
Single @ 30K income tax $4,500
Single @ 50K income tax $12,500
Single @ 75K income tax $18,750
Married @ 60K income tax $9,000
Married @ 75K income tax $18,750
Married @ 125K income tax $31,250

Source: www.taxfoundation.org/publications

The following is a list of taxes we did not have 100 years ago (a partial list and may vary by state): Sales tax, school tax, real estate tax, property tax, state income tax, corporate income tax, state unemployment tax, recreational vehicle tax, service charge tax, social security tax, federal unemployment tax, worker's compensation tax, Medicare tax, CDL license tax, road usage tax (truck drivers), food license tax, fishing license tax, hunting license tax, marriage license tax, luxury tax, inheritance tax, inventory tax, dog license tax, garbage tax, gasoline tax, fuel permit tax, accounts receivable tax, building permit tax, telephone federal excise tax, telecommunications federal universal service fund tax (e-Rate for public schools), telephone federal surcharge tax, telephone state surcharge tax, telephone local surcharge tax, telephone minimum usage surcharge tax, telephone recurring & non-recurring charges tax, telephone state & local tax, telephone usage charge tax, utility tax, environmental tax, vehicle license registration tax, vehicle sales tax, watercraft registration tax, and well permit tax.

Tax Freedom Day
The number of days employees must work to pay annual taxes

Year	Tax Freedom Day	Taxes as % of Income
1920	February 13	12.0%
1950	March 31	24.6%
1970	April 19	29.6%
2000	May 3	33.6%
2004	April 17	29.3%
2008	April 23	30.8%

Source: www.taxfoundation.org.

Myth 2: Large Corporations Are Evil And Control The World

This myth is an insecurity that stems deep from within the liberal personality. Michael Moore, film producer and liberal critic, epitomized this myth when he was being interviewed on Larry King Live by stating, "We must take the control of our country out of the hands of the rich corporations" (April 30, 2008). This obsession with corporations is a liberal paranoia. As we have learned with the Promoter Personality Style, one of their characteristics is they love to spend money; it filters through their hands quickly.

As a citizen in a free capitalist society, it surprises me how paranoid, naïve, and unrealistic those on the left are when it comes to business. If one analyzes it, within any business or corporation the most coercive and most potential area for deceit is the sales department. And, as learned earlier about personality styles, is that the Promoter is the natural salesperson. As anyone who has dealt with a salesperson, especially an aggressive sales person, they are not beyond bending rules to obtain their goals. This happened on a national scale during the writing of this book with the housing market (See, "Too Much Sensitivity & The Housing Collapse" in the Appendix).

The following saying gives good perspective to Myth 2, "Never attribute to corporate malice what can be explained by poorly thought out regulation." This summarizes the increase in white-collar crime, and the housing crisis which reached its height during the presidential election of 2008. Because of the sensitivity and strong belief in personal freedom and government, in a growing liberal society, laissez-faire and apathy occurs in many aspects of society.

With steady increases in energy prices, an ancillary to this corporate paranoia is the liberal belief that oil companies are receiving big profits, and that all their corporate executives are getting rich. On a corporate accounting sheet, if the corporation has a profit of even five percent after expenses it is considered fortunate. For oil companies a good portion of their budgets have to be utilized for costly exploratory drilling. When taken in the aggregate, the millions and billions of revenue the media reports for large corporations does not amount to anything that exceptional when the cost of doing business and overhead is brought into the balance sheet. A great portion of this corporate overhead is employee salaries and benefits.

Even understanding fundamental business and economics would put this in perspective. When you look at it empirically, a free market gives the consumer (citizen) more power than a democracy does. There is truth to the old saying, "you cannot fight city hall", but in a free market you can certainly refuse to buy a certain product, or boycott a specific company. Government and the free market run parallel to each other. But the free market is independent of government, and functions effectively, as long as government does not upset the balance with too much regulation, taxes, or interest rates. Business is generally honest and self-policing (*Better Business Bureaus, self-regulated trade organizations, etc.*), but things can get more complicated when it gets involved with Government Sponsored Enterprises (GSE), such as, *Fannie Mae and Freddie Mac.*

It has been said that if Congress were a business, all its members, at one time or another, would have been held on corruption charges. What Bernie Madoff did is miniscule compared to what the government has done, over time, to millions of its citizens. It is interesting to note that, "…over the past 45 years, the stock market (regardless of party) has risen 1.7 percent while Congress is in session -- and 17.7 percent when it is not."[1]

Myth 3: The Natural Resources Are All Being Destroyed, And Global Warming Is Going To Destroy The Earth

The function of the Earth can only be measured in millenniums of time. Mankind has only been civilized for the last 5,000 plus years. Given this information, it is impossible to determine where we are geologically. We are only now beginning to understand some of the things that have affected the Earth geologically in time. Ours is only an educated guess. There have been disastrous events that have occurred that have totally changed the development of the Earth. The Earth has been through global warming before, maybe many times in the past, and has continued to persist. It is speculative at best what millennial course we are currently on and to what degree mankind is altering this.

When you consider our own nation, ongoing immigration (whether legal or illegal) will put more and more strain on the environment. With the United States population being only five percent of world population, the potential for continuous immigration is great. This is another of the hypocrisies of the liberal psyche. They wish to protect the environment, but are against such economic endeavors that will better the lives of the masses; For example, oil drilling to help the energy crisis. And, at the same time, liberals are soft on immigration, which also affects the environment by adding ever more population to the already limited resources remaining in our nation.

Some are concerned about the carbon dioxide that is produced by mankind. Since we are looking at Earth cycles that take millenniums to complete, it is difficult to determine in our short observation of history where the Earth is in its cycle. This has been the case with global warming. It gets even more uncertain where we are in this Earth cycle when we examine our archeology, paleontology, and geology evidence of past ages. Scientists know the Earth is always in warming or cooling trends, depending on the interval of time being considered. It is always on a cycle, since the end of the last millennium the Earth has been cooling.

We are learning more and more about the Earth's geological history. There have been epochs that created what we now call *volcanic winters*. These are caused by a major volcanic eruption or large meteor strike, which causes debris to be put into the atmosphere which reduces sunlight, and therefore destroys vegetation. This in turn affects the rest of the food chain, and species become extinct. There is geological evidence this occurred with the mysterious disappearance of the dinosaurs 65 million years ago. This must have also occurred at other times over the four billion year history of the Earth. There are well over one hundred and fifty identified impact craters visible on Earth.

During the last tens of thousands of years there have been major volcanic eruptions. When each of these eruptions occurred it spewed more carbon dioxide and ash into the atmosphere than man has created collectively since our existence. The largest volcanic eruption in known history is referred to as *The Toba Catastrophe*[2], located on the island of Sumatra, in Indonesia at Lake Toba. It erupted about 75,000 years ago. The eruption occurred for over a week, and everything within 500 miles was destroyed and ash spread for 2,000 miles. The super volcano eruption created thick clouds of ash and sulfur gas which reached the stratosphere, and stayed in the atmosphere for a period of time causing global temperature change. Because of the diminished sunlight, the earth cooled by twenty degrees or more. This created several years of volcanic winter around the globe. Vegetation began to disappear which caused a collapse in the natural food chain, killing the majority of life on Earth. Within a few years this temperature change created an ice age which may have lasted a thousand years.

"According to the Toba catastrophe theory, the consequences of a massive volcanic eruption severely reduced the human population[2]." It is believed by scientists that over three million years ago, that human and ape lineages diverged from a common ancestor. This human stem-line produced several divergent lines. A theory proposed in 1998 by Stanley H. Ambrose at the University of Illinois, postulates that this massive volcanic eruption may have also critically reduced human population. This environmental change would have caused changes in, and extinction of the various lineages of man. It is proposed that only two lineages came out of this chaos. It is thought that these lineages became Neanderthals and modern Homosapiens (modern man). Present day Lake Toba, 60 miles long by 20 miles wide, is what remains of the volcanic crator caused by the Toba eruption. Super volcano eruptions can happen once every 100,000 years.[2]

Another event which affected world climate was in 1783 in Iceland, called the *Laki Fissure Eruption*. There were several days of volcanic fissure that spewed ash (an estimated 100 million tons) and sulfur dioxide into the atmosphere. A thick red haze hung over Iceland causing failed crops and the death of 75 percent of livestock. As the haze drifted over Europe it caused cooler weather and affected areas as far away as New Orleans. That year was one of the few known times the Mississippi froze over completely in New Orleans, and Japan had a colder than normal season which devastated many of its crops. The Laki eruption produced the largest lava flow (2.9 cubic miles) in recorded history and covered 218 square miles.[3]

Then there is the phenomenon referred to as the *Medieval Warm Period* [4] which occurred between 900 and 1300 AD (also referred to as the *Medieval Warm Epoch*). It was an era of warmer temperatures, which was immediately followed by a cool period called the *Little Ice Age*. This warming phenomenon occurred during the Medieval Period in Europe. Most of the documentation of this warmer period came from Medieval European record keepers. This climatic warming also accounts for the north Atlantic explorations that occurred during this era. The Vikings discovered and colonized Iceland, Greenland, and Newfoundland. These explorations were made possible because of reduced glacial activity, which made oceans freer of ice.

Temperatures begin cooling about 1250 AD, with the coolest time during the 16th and 17th centuries. By 1850 the temperature began to rise again. This increased temperature during the medieval period is similar to the increased temperature experienced during the early 1900s. There is evidence that increased sunspot activity caused these temperature increases, and that increased volcanic activity is attributed to the cool period called the *Little Ice Age*.

It is also interesting to note that Lake Superior, the world's largest fresh water lake, containing 10 percent of the Earth's fresh water, rarely freezes over completely, but has twice during the last decade. It occurred in 2003, and then again in 2009, with significant amounts of freezing already occurring in December of that year. Prior to this, the last time Lake Superior froze over completely was in 1979.[5]

It is natural that environments change, as do species. They must evolve or become extinct. It is not only the present that man has caused extinction of species, this has happened throughout history. It occurred when man discovered fire, more effective weapons, civilization, cultivation, domestication, and hybridization. It is only in recent times that we have sought to preserve species. Many species would have become extinct without our protection or domestication. But our protection is not a natural phenomenon; it is not what would happen in nature. The sensitivity of a culture has not spared or preserved species before. In essence, hundreds of thousands of species have become extinct throughout history. Species on the fringe of extinction will continue to be wards of our society. All through evolutionary history, one species has superseded another because of its better adaptability to changing environments and conditions. Human evolution and civilization has been one of those environmental conditions.

Carbon dioxide is an odorless and colorless gas constituting 0.04 percent of the atmosphere. For maximum plant growth green houses utilize three times this atmospheric level. Carbon dioxide is essential for plant photosynthesis and ultimately for all life on earth. We exhale about four percent carbon dioxide in our breath. In the last 200 plus years the carbon dioxide level has only increased by a trace amount. As already mentioned, the earth goes through natural processes of cooling and warming phases, and has since its creation. It is also evident when sunspots occur on the sun they create a warming effect on the earth. This explains why some years are warmer than others. Ironically, the atmosphere of the planet Mars consists of 95 percent Carbon Dioxide, yet it averages minus (-85) degrees below Fahrenheit (-60 degrees Celsius).[6]

With our human population in the billions and our endless production and manufacture of material goods, mankind has the potential to affect the environment. But, with our technology we have already minimized automobile and manufacturing emissions. We also overlook how much of the carbon dioxide is being absorbed by existing foliage and sea algae around the world. Global change of some sort is always going on, it is a continuous cycle. The renowned climatologist and professor of environmental sciences, S. Fred Singer, Emeritus at the University of Virginia, explained that, "The Earth is either always warming or cooling; one cannot tell which it is unless one specifies the time interval."[7] Mankind is only one small part of this change. It is presumptive to blame humanity when it is only speculative, and takes over a millennium to see any change.

Modern scientists have several theories about events that trigger global climatic change and glacial activity, these are considered to be: 1) astronomical variations in the Earth's orbit; 2) changes in characteristics of the sun (heating occurs during sun spot activity, or cooling during non-sun spot activity); and, 3) increased volcanic activity that spews ash and dust into the stratosphere which creates an insulated layer causing lowered temperatures on Earth.

My decades old college notes from an astronomy class also outline some of these causes: Every 22,000 years the Earth completes one "wobble" on its axis and the angle of the Earth changes by three degrees every 41,000 years. Every 100,000 years the Earth's orbit around the sun "stretches" (elongates), this causes a cooler climate because the Earth is farther from the sun for a longer period. Enough cool summers can lead to an Ice Age. The average yearly temperature during the last Ice Age, based on the area which is now Ohio, was 26 degrees Fahrenheit; the current yearly average has been 53 degrees.

As I consider human history, I am convinced that we will destroy each other before we destroy the environment. *The Discovery Channel* [8] with its series, "Life After People", portrayed how nature would take over if mankind were gone. Animals would run wild and vegetation would cover over everything. All human structures would eventually weather and collapse and be covered by dense vegetation.

Myth 4: We Never Spend Enough On Education

A finding of many surveys is that the American populous is increasingly dissatisfied with public education, and consequently, has caused an increase in private education and home-schooling. Students attending private schools are academically months ahead of their peers in public education, and the majority of private school students are also readily accepted to college. Government has at times introduced school-choice legislation where parents would be able to use a voucher, or increased education tax credit, to help parents with private school tuition. It was also found that utilizing a voucher system costs less than the per student fee for public education. This was especially true in the Washington D.C. school district. These programs unfortunately are not in the belief system yet of legislators. Those that believe in large government generally also believe in government control of education, even though many Senators and House members hypocritically utilize private education for their own children.

Unfortunately, many times education is used as a political tool. Education can become a controversial issue and the ready ammunition of an election. There are many unchanging issues in education. One issue is how we rate the effectiveness of public education. It takes years to see how well students have done. Input from educators reveals the biggest problem in education is that it is wrapped in politics and unfunded mandates. Mandates are rulings by Congress for changes to the practices of education, usually additions to, that Congress has made into law, but for which it has not considered any funding. It is up to the school districts across the nation to raise money through local property tax, or through their own revenue raising initiatives.

The early framers of this nation knew how limited it was for most American citizens to obtain an education. The Founding Fathers knew that only the aristocracy in British society was able to afford an education and how important education was for anyone to reach a comfortable level of society. But in America today, against the wishes and original intention of our Founding Fathers, public school and colleges have become left-of-center indoctrinated, not the even keeled institutions they were designed to be. The early framers of The United States would cringe if they knew the bias our students receive, the suppression of historic facts, the elimination of religion in our schools, and how much leftist indoctrination is done to students. These are the realities that have made parents move to alternative education resources. In many societies the option to seek alternative education or home schooling was forbidden. This occurred in Nazi Germany and the USSR. Today, communist states, suppressive dictatorships, and many Islamic states also deny this option. Germany to this day does not allow home schooling.

In theory, increasing per student funding would allow schools to hire more teachers, have smaller class size, more supplies, technology and resources. But statistically this has not been proven in itself a guarantee to raise academic levels. Student academic gain is the litmus test. Studies and research have proven education spending has not improved achievement. Just increasing spending on education does not obtain the academic results you wish. Such organizations as the *American Legislative Exchange Council* and the *Heritage Foundation* (both listed in the Appendix of this book) have done studies proving there is no correlation between increased per pupil spending and teacher pay, and, therefore, little correlation with student to teacher ratios for student improvement. Smaller districts in urban areas have shown some improvement without requiring more funds. And with any tax supported entity, results improve when citizens (parents) have choices and get involved. This makes providers more responsive individually instead of to bureaucratic accountability. Education should build character.

Spending per student has increased over time. We are at historic levels of spending on education. Consider the following:

Between 1984 and 2004 spending increased by 49%
Between 1994 and 2004 spending increased by 23.5%

Average per pupil spending 1919-20 was $354
Average per pupil spending 1970-71 was $4,060
Average per pupil spending 1999-2000 was $6,584
Average per pupil spending 2005-06 was $9,266
Source: www.Heartland.org.

At the 2005-06 rate of $9,266, a first grade student starting school in 2005 by 12th grade will have $111,192 spent on their public education (Heartland.org).

Part of the average per student cost is related to special education which is twice the cost than for the average student. The majority of school budgets are spent for more teachers due to increased class size and rising teacher salaries.

The premise of the *No Child Left Behind (NCLB)* initiative upheld by former President George W. Bush, was designed to improve student performance. There were many critics of the NCLB federal program. But what it did more than any other program was to make schools and educators more accountable. Therefore, districts would not lose the student to outside sources of supplemental education services, which would equate to a loss of district funds. Under the NCLB initiative, if a school does not make *Annual Yearly Progress (AYP),* parents can seek outside supplemental education resources from independent tutoring services or center-based supplemental education services such as Huntington, Sylvan, and Kumon. The district not meeting the AYP has to pay for these supplemental services out of its budget up to a specific amount per student.

Just prior to the NCLB initiative, charter schools were growing in school districts in response to the diminishing results of public education. Home schooling also saw a steady growth. The turn to private schools and home schooling was an alternative to those concerned about the neutralization and attitude toward religion (especially Christianity) in the schools, the overt socialization of public education, and because of a growing number of school shootings. About eleven percent of American students attend a private school. Private schools have distinct advantages. They have smaller classes, more school spirit and pride, and they have the peer and parental reinforcement to do well. In private schools there are less discipline problems, and a balanced curriculum that does not shy away from religious recognition. Many private schools also require uniforms, which maintain equality of dress and pride in belonging. Uniforms also eliminate peer competition.

According to the U.S. Census Bureau, in 2007, 29 percent of adults 25 years or older completed a Bachelor's degree.[9] Our national concern is that we keep up with other nations and cultures, especially in math and science. With oversensitivity and political correctness, we have totally pacified our schools. Our reluctance to uphold discipline and tough love have eliminated the only resources remaining for schools in this left leaning era, and therefore, schools had to establish zero tolerance policies. Education has also overextended its original intent with lunch programs, before and after school programs, etc. These additional budget concerns were never intended to become supported by districts. Education referendums, to offset the costs of these programs, are double-edge swords to property owners. Some states use sales tax, others property taxes. In many urban areas many people live in apartment buildings and pay little, if any, individual property taxes, but individual homeowners do. One of the largest cities in the state in which I reside has had three referendums pass in a row because of this disparity.

Parents need to have an active role in their children's education at all levels. They should attend school board meetings, voice their opinions on school and community issues, remain active in PTAs and PTOs, and form a concerned parents group – remember numbers get attention. Parents must be active in the events of their children's public education because their taxes are paying for it. You do not want those tax dollars to go to waste, or only represent a small fraction of the community. Parents need to be aware of the curriculum being taught to their children. This is crucial to know since the curriculum, and in many cases the politically correct dogma also taught, affect early socialization of school age children. This can adversely affect future culture. For example, in Mexico, until 1994, their school curriculum was teaching that the southern portion of the United States was taken from Mexico. Many Islamic schools in the Middle East still teach hatred toward Jews and Israel (See Chapter Ten, "50 Rules Kids Won't Learn In School" by Charles J. Sykes. The first eleven rules have been listed).

Myth 5: Government Is The Answer To Everything, It Should Take Care Of All Things

Our Founding Fathers purposely wrote the Constitution and the Bill of Rights to protect and make America beneficial to the individuals who built and made it strong. They pre-cautioned against large government.

The age old ideological difference between liberal and conservative is the treatment of government as a political base. As explained earlier, liberals feel government should be there to take care of their every whim. Those on the left are comfortable with large bureaucracy and are not opposed to paying taxes to support an expanded government. Conservatives, on the other hand, want government to be a minimal part of their life; to be there only for international protection, to maintain a criminal justice system, and to protect commerce.

In essence, anything that government can do, could also be done by the private sector. There are many examples of this. The Occupational Safety & Health Administration (OSHA) for example, could have been privatized. Private sector groups and companies are always more efficient than a similar entity established within government. School districts have utilized outside resources, as have communities and local governments throughout the United States. The saying goes, "If congress were a business it would be bankrupt", the truth is it would have been bankrupted over 200 years ago.

Unlike government, businesses must strive for efficiency. They must market their services to obtain and keep customers. I will never forget the comment made by a person standing in line at a local post office, during the time when the post office tried to be a functioning private corporation. Standing in the middle of a line of twenty five people, the man looked back at the ever growing line and said, "How can anything fail with this many customers waiting in line?" Large corporations that have done well have done so without the help of government.

Government influence on business and the free market only hampers their growth and survival. Continually raising taxes negatively affects the economy by ultimately reducing and eliminating jobs.

It is interesting to note that of the top twelve poorest cities in the United States with over 250,000 in population, that most have not elected a Republican mayor for twenty years or more. For several of the cities it has been closer to fifty years, and it has been 100 years for three of them; and two have never elected a Republican mayor. The citizens of these cities continue to elect Democrat mayors, but their poverty status does not change. This is easy to see from the following chart. Fresno is the only city listed on the chart with a Republican mayor. Because of its large agriculture industry, Fresno has experienced a continued influx of seasonal workers that affects its demographics and economy.

TOP 12 POVERTY CITIES WITH OVER 250,000 POPULATON

Rating	City & State	Persons Below Poverty Level	Last time Republican mayor has served
1	Detroit, Michigan	33.3%	not since 1962
2	Cleveland, Ohio	30.5%	not since 1989
3	Buffalo, New York	30.3%	not since 1965
4	Newark, New Jersey	26.1%	not since 1928
5	Miami, Florida	25.6%	no previous served
6	Fresno, California	25.5%	Republican elected
7	Cincinnati, Ohio	25.1%	not since 1980
8	Toledo, Ohio	24.7%	not since 1989
9	El Paso, Texas	24.3%	no previous served
10	Philadelphia, Penn.	24.1%	not since 1952
11	Milwaukee, Wisconsin	23.4%	not since 1908
12	Memphis, Tennessee	23.1%	not since 1910

Source: US Census Bureau, Poverty & Health Statistics Branch for 2008; and www.worldstatesman.org/US_mayors.html.

Myth 6: Republicans And Conservatives Are Cold, Insensitive People, Who Only Want To Become Rich

Liberals and Democrats don't have a patent or monopoly on sensitivity or helping others. Those on the left have disdain for the political right; they feel the right has no sensitivity. To a liberal it is all about sensitivity. But conservatives have a lot of sensitivity toward others. This is seen in their contributions, support of charitable organizations and their community. They have programs in place for the needy. The difference with conservatives is they use more fiscal planning and forethought with their sensitivity and compassion. Proper budgeting is accomplished and programs are designed for the truly needy. Conservatives are practical and look to data to make decisions, not just unsubstantiated emotion.

What liberals and Democrats do not stop to consider, is that conservatives believe in fairness and justice. A professor at Syracuse University, Arthur C. Brooks published, "Who Really Cares: The Surprising Truth About Compassionate Conservatism." In the book he relates, "Although liberal families' incomes average six percent higher than those of the conservative families, conservative-headed households give, on the average 30 percent more to charity then the liberal households. Conservatives also donate more time and give more blood."

A capitalistic system allows freedom of choice. It is based on ambition and the desire to get ahead. If you wish to do well, the opportunities are there. If you wish to live on the streets the opportunity is also there. But there are provisions in place and money budgeted and directed to help those truly poor, and those disabled (mentally or physically). We have a society of individuals that readily give and support charity with monetary donation and by volunteering. Through these charitable organizations and individuals, there is ready help available for those truly in need, and those that are temporarily in need. Liberal government does not need to incessantly raise taxes just to force everyone to a certain level – *c'mon you libs don't you believe in free choice*? Liberal political platforms believe in free choice, but insist on forcing everyone to the same socialist level, and do so through government redistribution. Socialism tries to force everyone to be equal. But the repeated failure of socialism and communism has proven it does not work.

Two of the riches men in the world, two Americans living in the United States, Bill Gates and Warren Buffet have given billions to charity. But the rich, and conservatives, Republicans, and successful business persons are still referred to as the *culture of greed*. The amounts of charity given by Mr. Gates and Mr. Buffet would easily surpass that of all the liberal members in Congress, if they would have given collectively since the beginning of our nation. Liberals are the ones always promoting that everyone else should pay more taxes and give more to their fellow man. To the liberal, it is always about everyone else paying, they are seldom the first to reach into their pockets, unless provoked to do so. This is another obvious hypocrisy.

An interesting study done at several Eastern Universities[10] found that conservatives are more disgusted and turned-off quicker than their leftist counterparts by more despicable and squeamish things. Participants were rated on how they reacted to such things as maggots, foul smells, body parts, and graveyards. Data was then compared, and it was found those most easily disgusted were more likely to be politically conservative. This was concluded as being nature's way of assuring self-preservation, safety, and avoidance of disease. Ironically, it was not found to be true of non-conservatives. They were not as easily disgusted by the same things. This may also help to explain why non-conservatives seldom jump ship when one of their own dishonors themself. In a separate, but related study at another university, it was found that those more easily disgusted tended to also be opposed to gay marriage, abortion, and issues related to morality. It is thought this characteristic of being easily disgusted evolved in humans to keep them from unsafe situations.

CHAPTER FOUR

HOW WE HAVE SLID TO THE LEFT

America has always been great when we have allowed ourselves to be great.
~ Ronald Reagan

Liberty means responsibility. That is why most men dread it.
~ George Bernard Shaw

I predict future happiness for Americans if they can prevent the government from wasting the labors of the people under the pretense of taking care of them.
~ Thomas Jefferson

People cannot explain how America has changed. They do not know why they are unhappy with society and government; how all these changes have occurred and why there is a disparity in responsibilities and respect for the individual. They give Congress some of the lowest ratings it has ever had because their representatives do not listen to their concerns. They are unhappy with the way America has drifted. They know it is a different world than what they were used to only decades before. In its infancy, liberalism began as a movement for individual freedoms and improvements, but through the years it underwent change, a change predominantly to the left.

What the citizenry is acknowledging is that the whole of society has shifted to the left; not just the liberal, but the moderate-Democrat. Even conservatives and Republicans have been swept up and gravitated more to the center, and beyond. There has been a complete shift. Our society has ventured to the left, now we are stuck in this liberal abyss. As the saying goes, "A rising tide lifts all boats".

With its ever-growing influence, liberalism has continued to circle the globe and has affected most geographic areas and cultures. What goes around comes around. A society cannot function effectively in only one continuous political pole. A society cannot continue decade after decade stuck in a liberal or conservative canyon. A society must be dynamic, and therefore, hover in the middle for its efficiency and long term survival. There have been few sustaining liberal societies in all of history. Even in nature there must be balance.

Many social changes occurred in America during the 1960s and 1970s, especially with voting age and military service. The idea was that if you were of age to go into the military, you should be able to also vote. The voting age was changed to eighteen years of age, and the military draft became voluntary. There was also emphasis on being able, as a citizen, to access government records, which had traditionally been limited to the public. At the same time, more opportunities became available for women and minorities. Dual family incomes began to change the economy as families had more disposable income.

Socialism is the reoccurring plague of humanity. Every new generation struggles with it. My father's generation had to defeat Adolph Hitler and his Nazi-Socialist state. The world had to go to war to stop Hitler. Russia, China, North Korea, Cuba, and several South American countries have struggled with socialism in past and current generations. Socialism always seems a simple solution to address the masses; to make all as one. A system espoused by Marx so that no one person would be hungry, lack a livelihood, or shelter. Indeed socialism supplies a basic institutionalized life, but that is all. The other side of socialism is that it quells entrepreneurs, individual ambition, self-respect and private ownership. We know that communism and socialism have failed, and liberalism only lasts until the money runs out.

Just as socialism had to be invented, so did liberalism. You do not observe these ideologies in nature. They had to be conceived and then put into practice. What most liberals and socialists do not admit is that there are inherent flaws in their ideology. First, liberalism and socialism take away individual will to produce. Secondly, there will always be a social elite in either one of these ideologies, as was obvious in communism. There will always be hierarchical oversight. But elites tend to be out of touch with their populous, just as Louis XIV was out of touch with the French people, which ultimately caused the French Revolution. Thirdly, under a liberal-socialist ideology, individual economic freedom is eliminated. When you consider the ideologies of totalitarianism, socialism, communism, and liberalism, all these political systems limit economic freedom. This is a crucial fact to remember. Too much government intervention and regulation always destroys freedoms. Nothing is ever free, there are usually strings attached and conditions that must be followed (this is one reason why most people are against government bailouts).

It is not possible to have unlimited liberty, a maximum amount of utility, and an unlimited range of choices at the same time. People don't escape from a democracy like they did from East Berlin during the era of the Berlin Wall (the Iron Curtain), when Communist Russia occupied East Germany. They wished to escape the limited freedoms of socialism. In the 1970s I visited the Eastern Block Soviet colonies of Eastern Europe, which were established by "Mother Russia" from the outcome of World War Two. This was long before the Berlin Wall came tumbling down. I was amazed to see how limited the storefronts were, and the long lines for just common commodities like toilet paper. Butcher shops would have delivery of meat once a week, which created long lines waiting for a fresh cut of meat. I was also amazed at the high percentage of alcoholism. Public drunkenness was obvious. The communist system had taken away the will and soul of the people, alcoholism was a good alternative to their humdrum regimented life.

The story goes, that once, a professor of economics, during his discussion of socialism commented to his students that he had never failed a single student, but once had failed an entire class. The class argued with the professor that socialism works because there would be no poor and no one would be rich; therefore, socialism would be a social equalizer. Having already given his points about socialism to a deafened class, the professor told his students that he would do an experiment. He explained that all grades in the class will be averaged and therefore everyone would receive the same grade so no one would fail and no one would receive an A.

After the first class exam, the grades were averaged and everyone got a B for their grade. The students, who studied hardest, were upset, but those students who studied the least were very happy. By the time of the second exam the students who had studied the least, studied even less, and those students who had studied the hardest, were disillusioned and decided they too wished to have a free ride, so they also studied very little. The average on the second class exam was a D, and no one was happy.

By the third exam the class average had sunk to an F, and the scores never increased because of the bickering and blame, causing hard-feelings, and no one would study for the benefit of anyone else, and to their surprise all failed. The professor's experiment proved that socialism ultimately fails because when the reward is great, the effort to succeed is great. But when government removes the reward, no one will try or want to succeed, and instead become demoralized. This is the real basis of how socialism functions.

As I have already mentioned, even the most socialist and communist states had an elite aristocracy, and always will have. This elitist group will become the new "culture of greed." They will live better than the "proletariat" they oversee. We can never escape the nepotism of the elite class, and in essence there will never be a true classless society because there will always be those in charge. Thus, liberalism is doomed to a cyclic existence (See, "The Socialist Spiral" in Chapter Two, and, "The Day America Stood Still" in the Appendix).

The full backlash against conservative culture did not occur until the affluence of the 1960s and 1970s. Prior to it, society was concerned with just making ends meet. We were still basically pioneer-spirited striving for the good life. It was not until the generation of the 1960s that this changed. More people were going to college, women were finding a new focus and new voice in society, which also begin to create dual family incomes, and thus more affluence, and there was an unpopular war raging in South East Asia.

With social changes it usually takes years to return back to a neutral balance. The liberalism that began in the 1960s ultimately resulted in reduced criminal sentences, and an explosion in social gifting and entitlement programs. These social changes were embedded in society during the 1970s; and the 1980s was a pivotal decade where older generation philosophies were losing out to new socialized directions.

We have never had a liberal society to this degree before. We really don't know its ultimate ramifications. We know that liberalism can function as long as we are in relatively good times, that is to say, *liberalism will work as long as there is money*. Entitlements and social gifting do not come without social ramifications. We know there is a small step from liberalism to socialism and communism, and that both have been historic failures. The best way to promote socialism is covering it in the cloak of liberalism.

A system that can parallel or incorporate the natural strengths and instincts of mankind produces the best results in any social environment or political philosophy. The system that best incorporates these natural instincts is a free market system. It is effective because the free market system takes into account the true nature of mankind which provides a self-correcting balance. George Washington commented that such a system as, "Governed by their [mankind's] own interests, and not by grander notions of what is good and what is noble."

For millennia people were governed by tribal chiefs and warlords, then peasants by feudal kings and monarchs, who gave them basic protection from other despots and demanded their servitude. Decisions of monarchs were final and expedient. Judgment was based on the individual monarch's personal experience, idiosyncrasies, and demeanor, usually not on impartial law. There was biased nepotism for family and descendant rule, creating dynasties. By the beginning of the 1800s, along with the growing Industrial Revolution, the concept of a socialist society began to take root. Especially among peasants and workers, who with long days of toil felt there was no hope for their betterment. By the mid-1800s socialism was cemented as an ideology by such persons as Engels and Marx. Liberalism grew from this.

Socialist concepts continued to grow, especially among those who had not done as well as others. This socialist ideology climaxed with Franklin D. Roosevelt's administration. With many social changes ushered in during his long tenure as President, FDR actually created what is now termed the *Welfare State*. Those on the left do not see liberalism as socialism, but as an extension of the rights they feel every citizen should have. Therefore, they ultimately see every citizen in the context of a welfare state, but the Constitution does not guarantee our rights to such social programs. Instead, the Constitution gives us free will to choose our destiny. It gives us the choice to be a productive individual, to make our existence better, or the free will to live otherwise.

With the liberal psyche soft on immigration and border control, and their concerns about hurting the feelings of illegal aliens, liberalism is already affecting our nation's security. If you are an illegal alien in our country you have broken the law. We cannot continue to save the world if our own security and future resources are at stake. With our current population at over 300 million, we do not have enough natural resources, or energy resources to continue pace with immigration, or the continued growth in our population just from the birth of new citizens. We need to be more critical on immigration, especially since Muslim fundamentalists have declared war on the non-Muslim world, and have since upheld their threat. These are issues that liberal government and society is soft on.

It is ironic in my state of Minnesota, in 2006, during one of the debates for governor one question asked was, "If the candidates for governor would condone the use of a tag to mark the license plates on vehicles driven by foreign nationals, who did not have citizenship in this country." Two of the candidates (Democrat Mike Hatch; and, Independence Party

Peter Hutchinson), adamantly would not condone this proposal stating it would "stand them out", but the Republican (Tim Pawlenty) running for governor, with no hesitation, said he would definitely condone this action. Liberals are resolute to protect a small class of non-citizens of the US, over the greater security of US citizens is shocking, especially since 9/11, the greatest act of terrorism to the United States, was still so prevalent in everyone's thoughts. Needless to say, the Republican was elected to the office of governor.

If a regime like communist Russia is able to realize that communism does not work, and then change back to a free, more capitalistic society, why cannot the liberal end of the spectrum realize when there is enough liberalism? They will never admit it. Our society has been touting liberalism for decades, almost as long as the *Union of Soviet Socialist Republics* (USSR) did. It is pure speculation that a liberal would ever have enough liberalism. And their demeanor to accept anything without question as long as it has been generated from government would not allow them to ever speak against it. For decades this unnerving trend has occurred in our nation.

The millennium generation did not grow up with the Berlin Wall and the threat of nuclear holocaust from a communist world power, the former USSR. They did not have the constant reminders on the evening news of how many people tried to escape communist held Eastern Germany. And the ongoing defecting of visiting sports teams from those socialist states. People do not risk their lives to escape a government unless it is intolerable to live under. Communism was an intolerable system with few personal liberties and freedoms. The state controlled everything you did and there was only one state party, *The Communist Party.* Therefore, you had no option but to live the best you could, or try to escape. We cannot socialize our freedoms.

The reluctance of liberals to refocus themselves on the individual, shrugging the greater democracy, and in the above example, the safety of many millions of US citizens just to protect a few, the author calls *Democracy Disintegration.* To explain it further, Democracy is self-governing by the majority. If you start being politically correct, which is one sign of a growing liberal society, and dwelling on the small percentages of groups at the loss to the majority, you in essence erode the rights and the wishes of the greater majority. This is a concern which has been commonplace in our society for decades. It tends to set a different standard, giving power to illegal aliens and such groups to the detriment of our democracy and rightful citizens.

My generation grew up with "Westerns." They were movies and series about the exploration and settling of the American West. Westerns had a simple theme – stand on your own, be courageous, and live with a strong sense of right and wrong. And there was always justice. Western movies were strongest in the 1940s and 1950s, and began to decline in the 1960s. When our attention turned toward walking on the moon and exploring outer space, and society was moving quickly toward the next generation and liberalism, westerns became less popular. As society turned to the left, the western movie values were subdued, and eventually disappeared from our American conscious, and on movie and television screens. Periodically a film producer tries to revive the western movie, but modern westerns are changed in form and will never have the same impact or popularity they once had.

By the 1970s this liberalism was reflected in television series, such as "M.A.S.H." and "All In The Family." Their anti-establishment message was clear. At the same time there were also movies which satisfied those that were of the previous generation, such as "Dirty Harry" (1971 debut) the police detective that got the job done, played by Clint Eastwood, and the "Death Wish" (1974 debut) series of movies starring Charles Bronson. These latter movies were the last of their kind as our society liberalized.

Also during the 1970s police dramas were popular. One movie, based on a true story, was the "French Connection" (1971). The movie centers around two New York City narcotics officers who stumble upon a large drug smuggling operation with a French connection. These were the days when the audience would cheer when the bad guys were caught, or when the cops survived a long gun battle. When *French Connection* was released, audiences in the movie theatres would shout or stand up in their seats during some of the scenes where the cops were victorious.

But only decades later under expanding and thickening liberalism, we lost our pioneer spirit and the difference between right and wrong became blurred. Just like the problems experienced in public schools, the many decades of liberal psyche has caused a lack of respect toward our police officers and school administrators. In a liberal society there is little impetus to take on individual/personal responsibility, but liberals are still very vocal about what are perceived as their rights and entitlements. This was especially obvious during the writing of this book with the large federal stimulus packages of President Obama. A caller to a local radio program called to share with the host a cute story about her daughter, who, while eating breakfast that morning ran out of her daughter's favorite cereal. The child responded to her mother, "We should get a stimulus package so we can buy much more cereal." Liberal government keeps sending the wrong message to our youth and citizens.

Think of two triangles next to each other with one turned on its apex. The one on its apex is the taxpayers who keep the government going; the other triangle, standing on its base, represents the growth of government, ever-widening toward its base. There is nothing left but an implosion to happen when there are no persons left to pay the bills of over-expanded government. The spirit of those who have been heavily taxed becomes broken and they no longer produce, or they flee the state or country for better opportunities elsewhere. The following chart illustrates this social implosion.

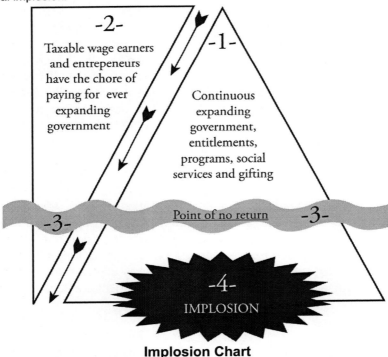

Implosion Chart
Result of Decades of Disproportional Society to the Left
1) Continuous growth of taxes, entitlements, government programs, social services, political correctness, nuisance laws and ever-expanding government causes a liberal abyss; 2) Those taxable wage earners, entrepreneurs, and corporations are given the chore of paying for the ever-expanding government; 3) At this point the disproportionate society will have to go to full socialism or communism, or implode into economic and social chaos; 4) The ultimate social implosion is wrought with chaos, social upheaval, economic strife, lawlessness, cultural degeneration, and vulnerability to outside influences (other nations, terrorism, and economic carpetbaggers).

CHAPTER FIVE

TWO WORLDS': THE LEFT AND THE RIGHT

A government big enough to give you everything you want, is strong enough to take everything you have.

My reading of history convinces me that most bad government results from too much government. ~ *Thomas Jefferson*

The best form of government is that which is most likely to prevent the greatest sum of evil. ~ *James Monroe*

As you have learned, Personality Styles ultimately reflect political platforms. Two major parties developed in the United States before the American Civil War, which created a polarized political environment. Our first constitutional President, George Washington pre-warned about the dangers inherent in political parties. The framers of the Constitution wanted to assure that government should be our servant, not our master.

As you are familiar with the personal characteristics of the Promoter Personality, let's magnify these characteristics into a national political base. Just as the Promoter Personality is single focused, so is the political left. Just like Promoters, liberals do not like to be bogged down in logic and fact, or criticism. They are also overly sensitive to others needs, to the point where they overdo things, especially tax-supported social programs. There was a book written about do-gooders, it explained how their efforts, however meaningful at the start, would come full circle and no matter how well meaning, always had a backlash that detrimentally affected those it wished to help. This is the thin edge oversensitivity can teeter on.

Politically, the age-old dilemma is that everyone wants more social programs, especially if they are low cost or free. However, few are willing to pay the additional personal taxes to support those services. This is true from school referendums to immigration programs. In a conservative world, individuals are expected to take more responsibility for themselves, and there is less need for as many social programs. In a liberal political existence, individuals expect government to take responsibility for their needs, and therefore, the government must tax accordingly. Liberals want freedom, but ultimately restrict themselves by government and socialization. Liberals' belief in government is so strong they become subservient to it. This is another major hypocrisy of the left.

Even though the Promoter Personality wants to have its freedom and a carefree life, it looks to government to supply its needs. This is because Promoters need direction and do not have the fortitude in themselves (remember the Personality Style Golf Game, the Promoter did not even finish the game). They believe, if government will help you with more of your personal things in life, then it is considered a good deal, especially if it is supported by the masses through taxes, and therefore, not out of your own pocket. The concept is, if each citizen pays enough taxes, they all will be able to benefit from government, and then will not have to pay that much as an individual, while still having the social services they want. The downside to this social conscience is that liberal politics usually goes overboard and gets out of control with its sensitivity and limited restraint. A good example, Democrats always want to raise taxes, even in good times.

Conservatives take a more realistic and serious approach to life. They believe more in themselves and not having government control their life. They believe in free market enterprise, and in economy and business with less government interference and bureaucracy. They wish government to have a minimal influence on their life. Conservatives are the ones that utilize balance sheets, data, and fact to make decisions and to analyze a situation. Because of this, conservatives have been described as, "the Voice of Reason." To a conservative, the role of government is to protect the rights of the people. Government should protect us with local law enforcement, to process criminals, right injustices, and prevent monopolies, and maintain a military defense against other nations and political entities. Therefore, conservatives in reality - have more freedom because they believe in themselves and rely on their own abilities. A quote, originally attributed to Thomas Jefferson, but changed over the years, "When a government tells you how to act, it is tyranny, when you tell the government how to act it is freedom", and Thomas Paine, "That government is best which governs [the] least", summarizes conservative principles.

Conservatives want limited government, liberals consider government a part of their existence. Liberals see government funded by the individual tax payer as their entitlement. It has been said, "To be a liberal is easy, but to be a conservative you have to work at it." The conservative will always have a disadvantage when it comes to elections. Many people see liberals as more social friendly and willing to empty the national treasury on them, and conservatives as absorbed by capitalism and business. Many on the left like to refer to conservatives as the *ownership society*. Liberals believe themselves to be superior to non-liberals, and better at solving problems than conservatives. This is perceived as arrogance by others. The liberal attitude about the general American public is that it is naïve and uninformed. That is why they feel that those on the left must make decisions for the "less fortunate" groups and classes, since they feel those groups are not able to do it themselves.

Liberals abhor conservatives. The liberal personality style feels very restricted by the conservative right. One only need read the rantings of Al Franken in his book, "LIES And The Lying Liars Who Tell Them," and other hard leftist liberals, to understand this. What we eventually conclude is that those on the far left are not very nice people. They are single-minded, self-righteous, and float more on emotion than on substantiated fact. Why do we continue to suffer so much from those on the left and their overt agendas?

What liberals really do not realize is without conservatives, there ultimately would be no liberals. Think about it. Liberals tax conservatives to support their agendas and programs and continue to float on the emotional and abstract, with limited accountability, order, or discipline. They would ultimately work themselves into chaos and disrepair. This is what is described elsewhere in this book as a *social implosion* (See, "Implosion Chart" in Chapter Four). You cannot support a liberal ideology without tapping monies from those that are working and productive.

To conservatives there is a line of common sense between what an individual should be responsible for themself, and what the community or government should do. Liberals feel there should be little individualized responsibility. Liberal society quells individual responsibility and at the same time creates heavy reliance on government. Too much government ultimately leads to socialism. Those on the left are collectivists, and until true socialism exists they will believe that America is a heartless and insensitive place.

Many times liberals appear overly serious and unhappy, because their unrealistic belief in humanity is constantly challenged. It is neither practical nor safe in today's terroristic world to be so overtly open and trusting. We do not exist in one big, happy, socialist world family;

we have inherent problems and concerns in our own society as well as in our global community. Liberals also tend to be serious because they cannot tell jokes to enliven things since they are oversensitized about offending others. They are too controlled by sensitivity and political correctness. Leftist sensitivity allows for little wiggle room; therefore, liberals are limited by what they can make jokes about or where to cast blame. Usually their sarcasm and satire is directed to Republicans and conservatives, especially towards white male conservatives. Many times sensitivity comes full circle to the liberal and makes everyone pay the price. The greatest example of this was the housing market collapse, where poor foresight caused a world economic crash (See, "Too Much Sensitivity And The Housing Collapse" in the Appendix).

Months after President Barack Obama took office, with a majority Democrat Congress, liberals still appeared unhappy and angry toward conservatives. Even when Democrats had a liberal President and a majority in Congress, where they were able to pass any bill, they were still complaining about conservatives. This unhappiness was baffling to many. One person explained that for eight years liberals had to contend with a conservative administration and could not pull themselves out of their critical mode. They were used to being angry, then things changed and their party captured the White House, but they still did not change their condemnation of everything right-of-center. They continued to find things to be angry about, similar to a sore winner phenomenon.

Then those on the left always need a crisis to motivate them, a cause to rouse them out of their *distracted air*. When their party gets in office they have no more crisis. Another person rationalized that with the whirlwind record levels of deficit spending that occurred almost immediately with the new Obama Administration, that liberals were actually concerned and fearful like everyone else for the future of our nation. But they hid these insecurities by continuing to criticize the former administration and conservatives in general. Others on the left may feel they needed to stay in the fight because of the initial treatment of their new candidate and party. They felt they needed to defend their candidate's new policies and administration.

It is the liberal's nature to be skeptical. Human nature consistently lets liberals down, which challenges their sensitivity and ideology toward their fellow human beings. The leftist psyche also tends to worry, has much envy, and does not tolerate opposing forces, especially when they hold power. They worry about forces that could change their status or situation. They also like to play the, "I'm more sensitive than you" game and need a scapegoat on which to put blame, i.e., the conservative. All these things compounded in the liberal's libido keeps them from being happy. One bumper sticker summarized it, "Annoy a liberal: work hard, save, be happy."

As a global community we interact with other nations and cultures. Many of these cultures and nation-states have different ideologies, traditions, and religions than us, which is usually not a concern for trade or international commerce. But, on occasion, a head of state gets elected that wishes to flex his nation's power, prestige, or land area with global neighbors. This is when international conflict can occur. Even though we exist in a globalized and integrated economy, it does not mean that all global neighbors are always going to follow the rules. Just as nation-states are extensions of human behavior, these behaviors can transcend to a global level. Just like a bully in the school yard is a part of the school global community, one must deal with that individual, just as other nations must deal with a nation with deviant behavior. Hence, there have been two World Wars and untold smaller conflicts.

Human society as a nation or political entity becomes progressively socialistic as it ages. First, new laws and regulations which are continuously being enacted over the course of time, contribute, ever restricting our social existence. The old army adage, "Always adding to, but never deleting from" certainly holds true in this case. Second, as populations grow the demand for social services also grows, which creates more reliance on government. We as a society have been moving to the left, and are reaching a saturation point -- we must move back to center. Unlimited government is not the solution, especially in a capitalistic infrastructure, just as Ronald Reagan said, "Government is not the solution; it is the problem."

We have traveled too far off-center in our society to the left. If we do not return to center soon, it will take many generations to offset the apathy and entitlement mentality we have created with the ongoing infiltration of liberal ideology and dogma. Increasing government is not the solution but becomes the problem. We have a national shortage of personal responsibility, totally opposite of our pioneer heritage. To the liberal faction of our society, government is security, direction, and personal power. Remember the characteristics of the Promoter Personality Style discussed earlier. The Promoter wants security, suffers from need of direction, and loves the limelight and power. With power and other people's tax money, they fulfill their need to have free choices and do what they want through government. Those that believe only in government for solutions always pay the price.

THE MEDIA DOUBLE STANDARD

Remember the childhood quip, "What is black and white and red all over?" Answer: a newspaper! I was instructed while growing up that you should believe nothing of what you hear, and half of what you read. Unfortunately, neither holds true anymore. Nowadays the media is a mastermind of taking things out of context. Just through sound bites, the liberal media can destroy an individual, a family, a business, an organization, or industry. The media does not have a conscience, especially when it comes to reporting on conservatives. "Let the dominoes fall," says the young journalist reporter who only wishes a name for himself through creating media hype and sensationalism, keeping alive the old journalist cliché, "If it bleeds, it reads."

Journalism, by its very nature should be non-opinionated, dispassionate, and report only the truth as it happens without bias. Media should be investigative so the truth is unraveled before it is reported to the general public. Media stories should follow a protocol. There is first the initial story, then the investigation for credibility before being dispensed to the media or press. This is considered good, unbiased, fair reporting. When it comes to allegations with our public servants, the media needs to ask serious, direct questions and investigate. News reporters should be detached and objective, and not protect public figures.

Just as the nation began its slide to the left in the 1960s and 1970s, the news media did also. As older reporters and media personnel, with traditional media standards retired and attrition took its normal curve, they were replaced by younger, more left-of-center idealists. It was the age of growing liberalism and these young reporters grew with it. They eventually became editors and brought with them their leftist views. Thus the age of liberal dominated mainstream media was ushered in.

In the United States, in today's media, nothing is reported without bias or double standards. One talk show host, Sean Hannity of FOX News stated that, "Journalism is dead in America." America is starving for unbiased media! It is sad when the people of our great nation have to go to special websites to verify that what the media is saying is true. Our biased media will be compromised when newspapers take their last fall and all our news becomes fully interactive electronically. Only then will the bias shroud of the media be overshadowed because every individual will have their say on every issue.

I am sorry to again use former President Clinton in my example. But, the one thing that I noticed, time and again, with the liberal as opposed to the conservative view, happened with the Clinton and Bush administrations. When in office, whenever President Clinton took some personal time off, the news media always referred to it as, "Some needed time off" or, "Well deserved vacation." Not so with either Bush administrations, they would, instead, stress the number of times President Bush had already been to Camp David with a demeaning tone. For senior or junior President Bush, the media condemned them in their rhetoric whenever either took any personal time off. The same courtesy given to Clinton was not given to George Senior or Junior because they were not Democrats. Why, you ask. One reason is because there are many liberal Promoters also in the media. Promoters are attracted to the limelight, the center stage, but unfortunately they also bring their liberal views with them so we receive biased news. What pressing issues did President Clinton have in any comparison to the administration that George W. Bush had on a daily basis, to warrant this disparity in treatment? With the war alone in Iraq, it was a 24/7 job for President Bush. Clinton on the other hand, did not have anything near the administrative decisions in his administration, until of course, the Lewinski case broke loose.

Also during the time George W. Bush was president, whenever his administration issued a terrorist warning, the media accused him of "fear mongering." In this respect, the bias media could have been the indirect cause of many American lives. Not so when the Obama Administration came into power. If President Obama's Administration issued a terrorist alert, the media gave it serious coverage and dissemination. How can media reporters be so biased as to put their fellow Americans in jeopardy, just because the current administration in power is not their political choice? What a low level we have reached in our media. This is why I feel there needs to be some kind of discourse taken against news media for not legitimately reporting or distorting the facts, because of the potential loss of life due to their bias.

As I have mentioned elsewhere, liberal reporters and media look at the ground when a Democrat gives in to his lack of morality. Reporters do not stigmatize them in the media. It took the media a while to highlight the Lewinski case. *The Drudge Report* was the first to acknowledge it. The mainstream media wanted the story but not necessarily against a sitting Democrat president. This does not hold true when a conservative or Republican is caught in an uncomfortable situation. I guess, because the right is expected to maintain a moral standard, they are scrutinized more by the media when they do not. Because the media accepts the lack of morality by Democrats, they do not consider it newsworthy when such events occur to a Democrat. The events are only reported to prevent competition by other news media reaching the airwaves with the story first. The liberal media has been doing this disservice for many years.

In the early 1980s when society was in its big drift to the left, we as a nation were still maintaining some etiquette. As mentioned earlier, this is what Gary Hart found out when he was discovered by the media (the not complete liberal media at the time) and photographed with a young lady in the Caribbean, while his wife remained home on the continent, unaware. Needless to say, this ended his career. If the same incident would happen today, the public would be apathetic and turn their heads, and probably elect him anyway. If he were a Democrat, the liberal media would dismiss it, play it down, and give it little coverage. Examples of this are obvious, and played out in the daily news. It is the age of sound bit manipulation. Only a few decades before this writing we criticized the Soviet Union for its manipulation of its media, now it's a daily event in our own media. We do not get the truth or full story from our media, only what liberal biased reporters and editors want us to see and hear.

The Republican Richard Nixon, Democrat Bill Clinton, and a host of others throughout US Presidential history, should have spent time under house arrest with those fancy electronic ankle bracelets for what they did to the presidency and to the people. At least Nixon had the fortitude to resign, Bill Clinton should have. This shows how our society has slid to the left. What would have been a disgrace for the office of the president two decades prior, when public sentiment would have made the president step down, is now accepted. In 1973, the people were calling for the head of Richard Nixon, but only a few decades later, when Clinton was involved in his sex scandal and blatantly lied to the American people on national television, the populous was apathetic. Clinton had sold them out as president and they went about their business as usual. This shows the apathy of our society. The presidency should be upheld with honor, good principles, credibility, honesty, and faith in a higher power, as seen in our Constitution. The American populous, overall, and none of the liberal arm, really realizes the impact for the future that the Clinton-Lewinski case has put on us. As a nation, it gave the presidency a new standard – and a much lower one at that.

Democrats have an advantage when it comes to elections because of the support they receive from the liberal media. This bias of the media is especially prevalent and obvious during local and national elections. Just paging through the headlines of a newspaper or online media, it is obvious by the placement of the article and the attention and coverage given to it. It is easy to see that the biased media has a propensity to give better coverage and credibility to liberal platforms. This was quite obvious during the 2008 presidential campaign. For several weeks the media purposefully referred to Governor Sarah Palin as Mayor Palin, instead of her current status and rightful title of governor. This was quite obvious, and stupidly humorous that the liberal media would be so blatant, and go to such a level, in their protection of a Democrat candidate for President, who in essence had less experience than did Sarah Palin as governor. And Governor Palin was only running for Vice President! It was ironic how much negative press she got because she was a threat to the frail egos of the liberal Democrats, and to an inexperienced presidential candidate.

It was a poor day when national elections began to be televised. It took the concern for issues away from the candidates and doomed them to Hollywood roles. The younger looking candidate automatically had the advantage, as did the smooth talking personality style, even if they would potentially lead the nation down a shaky road once elected. It has since been a ratings game for the media. The more charismatic candidate, regardless of ability, always has the advantage on national television.

Tax day, April 15, 2009, was a day of Tea Parties taking place in over 600 cities in the United States. These parties swept the country in response to the unprecedented debt and tax increases of the Obama Administration. At the largest Tea Party in the state of Minnesota which was held on the grounds of its state capitol, attendance estimates were over 3,000. Ironically, on the evening news that same day, and on media outlets the next day, the event was down-played by the media to suppress its significance. The media reported only about two to three hundred had gathered to support the concerns of taxation. In the evening newscasts only seconds were given to the event, and two out of the four predominant public television stations in the area did only a brief aerial view at a distance so protest signs could not be read.

Taxation is an age-old concern in American history and has been an important consideration to our freedom. It has been a special concern more recently with never before levels of federal spending and a budget deficit that will indenture all the next generations. It is an issue that primetime media should give unlimited coverage to so its viewers (citizens) are informed, but that is not the case with liberal biased media. The public is told what the media wants them to hear and see, and potential voters are led like sheep to heavy tax indenturement and socialist agendas. This is exactly how the liberal Democrat, through smoke screen and rhetoric, continues to lead the populous (sheep) to socialism. Our media is becoming more and more like that of the former Soviet (Russian) newspaper and media machine, *Pravda*. We have made several steps backward in our press and media. For the media to disavow all the warnings about government from the early framers, and not be a watchdog of government, at the least is dangerous.

It is ironic that during the writing of this book, all the information, cell phone conversations, witnesses and participants, photos, and information from public record, that the media was able to source about Tiger Woods and his many affairs. But yet the media is reluctant, and protective of President Barack Obama. With the investigative resources the media can muster, it should be able to unravel and find the truth to the legitimacy of President Obama's true hand-written birth certificate, college thesis and records, and associates, how his college was paid for, and what countries' passport he used when traveling in the early 1980s. This is a disservice to Americans and the Constitution of the United States. If there was a conservative President with questionable credentials, the press would be screaming for his head. Why would a news industry protect someone to the point of potential debasement of the United States Constitution and our security?

The media needs to return to its pre-liberal base and report the news as it is, unbiased and unopinionated. News reporters do not have the right to sway the news. It should be presented as it is, with the individual listener making their own conclusions. Reporters should not have a comment on the news they report, no innuendos, or facial or body language to sway the populous. How can we return a well implanted national liberal media system to a fair and balanced state when it always hides its liberalism behind the First Amendment?

We need to know when our candidates or elected officials are flawed, and it is the duty of the media to do so. Our biased media is no better than many of the politically quelled newspapers in socialist countries.

THE FUTURE OF THE MEDIA

What a biased media does is put mistrust on itself and on the liberal government that it espouses. The national media is the most biased. Newspapers and magazines will continue to have a lesser role. Only community newspapers will survive the changing times. Greatest emphasis will continue to be on the internet where individual bloggers can give their opinion. This individualistic involvement via the internet is a natural offset to established biased media. The internet not only allows the use of text, but audio, video, and graphics to enhance its delivery. A multimedia platform is very effective and will reduce market share from radio and television. The liberal hold on conventional news media will be limited.

How much lower can the media stoop? How long will we let them get away with consistently swaying the events just to boost ratings, or back their candidate? The biased, liberal media can elect you president or destroy you and your family. The only way this bias will be corrected, is by finding a way to make this disparity in news reporting a social injustice and treat it accordingly. Media organizations and journalists always hide behind the First Amendment even when their biased news reporting destroys a family, a business, or a community. This bias and power of the media must stop, and until we can bring it into the courts and win, it will continue to plague us. Again, the masses must speak out. I hope the intelligence level of America is not judged on the unscripted questions asked by media reporters.

CHAPTER SIX
HOW WE CAN BREAK THESE BONDS OF LIBERALISM
THAT HAVE STRENGTHENED OVER THE PAST DECADES

You cannot help the poor by destroying the rich. You cannot strengthen the weak by weakening the strong. You cannot bring prosperity by discouraging thrift. You cannot lift the wage earner up by pulling the wage payer down. You cannot further the brotherhood of man by inciting class hatred. You cannot build character and courage by taking away people's initiative and independence. You cannot help people permanently by doing for them, what they could and should do for themselves.   *~ Abraham Lincoln*

Bear with me. In writing this book, I am not a socialist, communist, Marxist, fascist, or liberal. I would ideally like to hover in the middle with a strong third party. Karl Marx wrote at a different social, political, and economic time in history. He wrote when socialism and communism seemed the only solution for the masses to all be at one level and not have any worries about having the basics of life (water, food, shelter, livelihood, etc). Marx was one of the authors of this philosophy, and whose book got into the ideological hands of such historic despots as Lenin and Hitler. The only thing Marx may have been right about is that you need to have a revolution (a drastic social stimulus) before any permanent change will occur. Unfortunately, Hitler, Lenin, and many other dictators utilized this strategy with militia.

In the case of liberalism, I am not promoting that we have street battles, but, I am saying we need an immediate awareness of the abyss we are in. We need to broadcast this so the populous is informed and we can make change. We have lost our pioneer spirit, this has affected our culture. What is also disconcerting is that a liberal society is easy prey to terrorism and outside forces. Because of the liberal-social abyss we are in, our culture has experienced drastic change.

Remember the Promoter Personality needs and does better with guidance -- left on its own it will continue to make decisions based on emotion, the trend of the day, other people's money, and more socialistic pursuits. As we have learned, liberals never know when there has been enough liberalism. This is especially true when our president is a Promoter Personality. This was the case with former president Bill Clinton; he had all the characteristics of the Promoter; he was indecisive, consistently needed help to make decisions, and had emotional breakdowns when countered or questioned as to wrongdoing, or from actions caused by his personal compulsiveness. It is fortunate that Mr. Clinton was president in a benign time; otherwise, the outcome could have been disastrous. Yet, as a Promoter he was still able to convince half the population with his rhetoric.

This is why a Promoter personality is a poor choice for such a position. Remember, in a corporate setting the sales department is but one department, usually overseen by a vice-president, who in turn is overseen by a president, and the president overseen by a chairman of the board. Even with a checks and balances system, you do not have control over the compulsiveness of a Promoter Personality type president. It is ironic that liberals still believe that putting your life on government is better, and that corporations are evil. The book by Rich Lowry, "LEGACY: Paying the Price of the Clinton Years" is one of many books unveiling the lack of leadership in Washington.

We get lost in the liberal hype. It is sold to us and to our children in schools across the nation and by the liberal media. It is as though we have been brainwashed with its messages of, "Build large government for assurance that it will take care of you", "Don't rely on yourself, rely on the aggregate", "Use taxes to feed government and thus give us security", and, "Build entitlements at every social level to help us rely on ever expanding bureaucracy."

As I have mentioned earlier, there can never truly be a socialist or communist society because there will always be an elite. Even in the former *Union of Soviet Socialist Republics* (Russia) there was a well defined social elite who enjoyed the benefits not available to the masses. Karl Marx would not have approved of this disparity within a socialized system. This is another hypocrisy within a socialist system. There are also many rich liberals that live the good life. As mentioned in a previous chapter, if they were true to their party platform, they would give away much of their wealth and become equal citizens, and live at the same means as the masses. This Karl Marx would have expected. In the Democrat Party in America, the rich Democrats are the elite.

The only way to overcome this liberal abyss we are in is to take back America. The "Hippie Revolution" started the lunge to the left and it progressed throughout the aging of the Hippie era "baby-boomers." A conservative social revolution, returning to responsible principles and judgment based on fact and reality, is the only way to spark society back to center. Individuals need to stand up for personal rights, individualism, and keeping government to a minimum in our life. We need to regain what we can of the pioneer spirit that has been left along the side of the road. To keep this lunge to the left from happening again, we need a strong middle party.

- **WE MUST EDUCATE AND AROUSE THE POPULOUS.** In this way, everyone will know what is happening politically and socially, and learn about the internal (socialism) and external forces that wish to destroy our existence (fundamentalist terrorism). Above all, we must stay educated and informed as to what is happening around us politically and socially. Be knowledgeable about political appointments and candidates running for office, what their position is on issues, their background and history, and who they associate themselves with. Thomas Jefferson said it best, "Anyone who expects to be ignorant and free expects what never was and never will be. Ignore your rights and they will go away", and also, "Enlighten the people generally, and tyranny and oppressions of body and mind will vanish like evil spirits at the dawn of day."

It seems many changes in Congress do not readily get disseminated to the average citizen. This is a flaw with our media. The government has supplied many sites to obtain information about its legislative agenda. The majority of the information is available, although at times tedious to gather and understand. To educate the public about candidates, policies, new rulings and mandates, used to be the role of journalism. Citizens need to be informed of all changes. This requires self-education of events and issues, but the media and government needs to have a better and more overt dissemination of these important changes. Especially since we learned during the Obama Administration, when healthcare was being debated, that Congress does not even read the bills it votes on. Do research on candidates running for office. Learn about their history and background, and voting record, and educate yourself on current issues moving through Congress. Support the elected office holders that you believe in, financially and through volunteering.

No matter how well we reform campaigns, it all boils down to the individual voter educating themself. When it comes to politics, and political and economic issues, what the citizen does not know or has not taken the time to learn, nor the interest to understand, could fill a major database. Most voters feel overwhelmed by the overall process, and feel their one vote will do nothing to affect the electoral votes. It always helps to return to grassroots levels. Each family should allow at least an hour a week to discuss current events and political issues as a family, just as you devote an hour a week to church.

The United States is still the greatest nation on Earth! If persons running for office do not believe America to be the greatest and best nation in which to live, and put it down through their rhetoric, then, *definitely do not vote them into office.* They obviously do not understand America, are very naïve to the rest of the world, or have an alternate agenda for America. They will be untrustworthy in office. We need to be watch dogs and keep these persons from gaining power.

- **PEOPLE NEED TO VOTE, VOTE, VOTE!** We need to vote in every election. The only way we are going to offset this liberal abyss we are in is by bringing this nation into the "middle." We need to take individual initiative and responsibility. Make your voice heard, do not be afraid to speak out. You have rights; our Constitution guarantees us individual rights.

Do not let a biased media or left-of-center following convince you that the left is the way to utopia. It is no better a direction than is the extreme right. Stand up for what you believe in, even if it is not popular and contradictory to the status quo. You are the paradigm; the future will ultimately go your way. Remember, the majority of the populous, if given the opportunity without overt influencing forces will select the middle of the political spectrum. That is where our society should remain, a fair and equal position for all, and keep extremists from disseminating their influence. "Don't just be a spectator in life" (Anonymous).

- **BE EMPOWERED AND STAND UP FOR YOUR RIGHTS!** Speak out, take on personal responsibility, write letters, email and blog; do not let the government suppress your free will and freedom of speech. Be "the squeaky wheel." It is not easy at first but you will get respect from others for your courage and principles, and eventually others will emulate you. It takes guts and a belief in yourself to stand alone – that is why there are not as many people who stand alone and speak out. People follow those that lead. Remember, just like the Promoter Personality, liberal politicians do not like to be challenged. This is true especially when they are wrong or not speaking for the majority, and when presented with statistics and data to disprove them.

We must step out of our molds and take risk. Decades of liberalism have molded us into this benign walking clay substance with no individual thought. It takes courage and fortitude to stand up for yourself – a lot of people find this difficult to do. Remember, "One man with courage makes a majority" (Andrew Jackson); "We must be the change we wish to see in the world" (Gandhi); and, "Don't let others stop you from doing what you know is right" (Fortune Cookie).

Those that receive the benefits of a generous society need to be accountable for their actions. Case in point, drug screen those taking public assistance to assure that our tax money is not promoting ongoing drug abuses. This will have ultimate positive benefit to the mother, her family, and set her children on a brighter course. We must all be the ready watchdogs of our government and its policies. Make our legislators and politicians accountable for their actions. As citizens we are accountable for our actions. In a liberal society many things are overlooked or tolerated in the name of sensitivity. But when a person accepts public office or aid, they should be just as accountable as any other citizen. Politicians with questionable anti-American affiliations or background should not be allowed to hold any political office, especially as a president.

As a citizen, you must stand up for your principles. Support organizations and institutions that uphold individual rights and personal freedoms. "To sin is silence when one should protest; makes cowards out of men" (Wilcox); and, "All that is necessary for the triumph of evil is that good men do nothing" (Edmund Burke).

- **WE NEED TO ESTABLISH A STRONG THIRD PARTY**. This will give citizens another option and balance. This would help keep society closer to center, not far left or right as a nation. A strong third party constitution should be drawn up and followed specifically as an independent political party base, with emphasis of avoiding the mistakes made by the right or left. I have devoted Chapter Nine to the discussion of a third party.

- **TERM LIMITS, EARMARKS, "PORK-BARREL SPENDING", LOBBYISTS, AND SPECIAL INTERESTS.** We need a cleanup of our existing government. We must impose term limits for all elected officials and the President. *All federally elected officials including the president should be one-term, and those terms should not be any longer than four years.* The problem with longevity is if too long in office, a candidate starts to believe that the public money is theirs and they become more fiscally irresponsible. This is seen in the growth of earmarks (*Pork Barrel*) trends. From 1991 to 2009 $290.3 billion was spent on 100,849 *earmark projects.* "While the number of specific projects declined by 12.5 percent, from 11,610 in fiscal year 2008 to 10,160 in fiscal year 2009, the total tax dollars spent to fund them increased by 14 percent, from $17.2 billion to $19.6 billion (Citizens Against Government Waste)."

Year	$ in billions	# of projects
1991	3.1	546
1994	7.8	1,318
1997	14.5	1,596
2000	17.7	4,326
2003	22.5	9,362
2006	29.0	9,963
2009	19.6	10,160

Source: Citizens Against Government Waste (www.cagw.org).

We need to rid our politics of special interest groups and influences. Representatives need to listen only to their constituents and their own conscience. We may also consider unicameral government for efficiency. With technology and population redistribution, small states will still maintain fair representation. The Senate has the worst reputation, their jurisdiction of a state-size area and population keeps them from being close to their constituents. I believe one House of Representatives would make for less costly, and more efficient, and effective government. We will obviously have to re-evaluate amendments to the Constitution and the power of the states to institute these landmark changes through a Constitutional Convention. The existing Congress will not address these issues.

Five Longest Serving Senators

Senator & Party	Service dates	Length of service
Robert C. Byrd D-WV	1959 - 2010	51 years 5 months
Strom Thurmond D>R-SC	1954 – 2003	47 years 5 months
Daniel K. Inouye D-HI	1963 to writing of this book	47 years
Edward M. Kennedy D-MA	1962 – 2009	46 years 9 months
Carl T. Hayden D-AZ	1927 – 1969	41 years 11 months
John Stennis D-MS	1947 – 1989	41 years 2 months

Source: www.senate.gov/senators/biographical/longest_serving.htm.

It should be a concern to all citizens to know that incumbent politicians at the federal level have a 96 percent re-election rate, and those at the state level a 92 percent re-election rate. This must end as a way of life for elected politicians. We must reinstitute common sense and fiscal responsibility in our legislators and representatives, and they must learn when to draw the line, otherwise, America will eventually be compromised. We can start this process by *consistently voting out all incumbents.*

With the explosion in communication and technology, we have made our society more efficient and timely. Effective decisions can be made by fewer elected officials, more effectively, and quicker. The framers of the Constitution could not fathom what America would be like 200 plus years later, but they had the foresight and fortitude to anticipate future challenges and changes. The first senators, until 1814, received up to $6.00 a day per diem (reimbursements for food, lodging, and miscellaneous expenses while on legislative business), by 1815 they were receiving $1,500 annual salary. We should seriously ponder a unicameral government. A smaller government would be less costly and more efficient. Consider the following data to 2009:

House of Representatives[1] The annual salary base per House member *$174,000 x 432* members = *$75,168,000.* Staff allowance per House member averages *$1.3 million x 435 = $565,500,000.* The Speaker of the House salary is *$223,500* + House Majority and Minority leaders are *$193,400 (x 2 members) = $610,300.* Total annually for House *$641,278,300!*

Senate[1] Annual salary base per Senator *$174,000 x 98* members = *$17,052,000.* Staff allowance estimate per Senator *$3 million x 100 = $300,000,000.* Senate Majority & Minority party leaders *$193,400 (x 2 members) = $386,800.* Total annually for Senate *$317,438,800!*

Per Diem[1] Estimated near *$3,000* per occurrence for member of congress and staff, even using a conservative guess of 300 trips annually x *$3,000 = $900,000.* **Retirement**[2] In 2006, 413 retired members of congress received *$22,103,976.* **Earmarks annually**[3] (House & Senate average of last five years) = *$21,260,000,000 billion.* To keep both houses going per year cost tax payers **$22,241,721,076 billion!**

In addition to the above, there are many other benefits members of Congress receive, many perks that are not publicized. Because they are required to maintain a residence in their home state, all their expenses are deductible while they are in Washington. They receive free franking privileges for letters and packages so they do not have to pay postage out of their budgets. Congressional per diem does not require itemized statements, and therefore is not closely monitored. Any remaining cash is supposed to be returned to the treasury. Also, costs for congressional overseas travel are not made public because it is lumped together into other budgets. Members of Congress are only required to report total per diem reimbursements received in cash for lodging, meals, and local transportation expenses. In the private sector, most businesses require itemized expense reports with attached receipts before they are reimbursed.

It is not unusual for Congress to have thousands of days in any one year spent overseas, all taxpayer funded. What is ironic, at the writing of this book, during the traditional August Congressional recess, there were eleven Congressional delegations that traveled to Germany. One questions some of these "fact finding" trips of Congress, especially since they have little oversight. Members of Congress and their spouses also fly free on military aircraft. A disgruntled citizen once commented, "We pay their [Congress] six figure salaries with our five figure salaries."

Members of Congress only need five years of service to retire at 80 percent of their highest salary. They are eligible for a pension when they reach age 50, if they have completed 20 years of service, or at any age after 25 years of service, or reaching age 62. Since 1984, members of Congress have been covered under the same plan as all other federal employees, the *Federal Employees Retirement System (FERS)*, funded by taxes and member contributions of 1.3 percent of their salary into the fund. In addition, they are required to pay 6.2 percent of their salary in social security taxes (based on data from 2009).[2]

Members of Congress can also earn up to fifteen percent of their salary with outside income, and there is an annual cost of living increase every January 1st of a new year, unless Congress votes not to accept it. As taxpayers we must work many more days of the year to pay for our government than what Congress is actually in session. There is no reason why we cannot permanently reduce some of our burden of government. Government does not even collect many of its own taxes it makes businesses and local counties do that for them.

In addition to a reduction in government, and Senators and their staffs, it would also automatically reduce earmarks, which in itself would be an estimated savings of $15 billion to taxpayers. Members of Congress also receive full pay when they are on the campaign trail. It was only during the writing of this book that expenses were posted for Congress for public view on the internet. Ironically, during the Constitutional Convention, Benjamin Franklin proposed that representatives not be paid for their service, but Franklin's proposal was quickly overridden. All members of Congress should be required to publish their tax returns each year as a public record. As President Harry S. Truman so eloquently put it, when referring to presidential responsibility, "The buck stops here."

The left likes to demonize business, but when the economy is down, companies cutback and downsize and revamp their business plans. They must do this to survive and keep stockholders happy. Businesses have to make cuts, reduce staff and make tough decisions during challenging times, there is no reason why government cannot do the same. If the government was run more like a business, it would be efficient. Each citizen is a stockholder of its government; however, those in elected positions in state and federal government do not have the same accountability as business does to its stockholders.

We see corruption on both sides of the aisle in government, especially among multi-term senators and representatives. No party is beyond corruption in its members. If they do wrong, these members need to be admonished and brought to justice so our government remains respectable and upstanding. Instituting term limits would be a great step in the right direction (See, "Representation" in the Appendix).

Little permanent change will occur until Congress has a shared fate with its constituents, and when they are consistently voted out after only one term. Government has been referred to as the *greatest Ponzi scheme*.

- **POLITICAL CAMPAIGNS.** We must assure that our basic right as citizens is not violated. All exit polling should be eliminated. There should be a media blackout during election days and results should be reported only at the completion of elections so voters will not be unfairly influenced. We must protect the process from error and fraud.

With advances in technology, there may be a time that individual citizens can vote on specific issues in the convenience of their own homes; therefore, citizens would have direct input on each issue. Obviously safeguards would have to be in place for such a system to be viable. This would bring more decisions down to citizen level.

- **EXCESSES AND MORALITY.** Excesses create greed. We need to clean up and keep politics clean. As a society, we must be good stewards for what God gave us. We should live with moderation; too much of anything is not good. We must be responsible individuals, community members, and citizens. Individuals and groups must take responsibility for themselves. We should be enraged and ready to impeach, and proceed with criminal justice when corrupt acts occur in government, and especially in the oval office by a President. Elected persons are responsible for upholding the Constitution. They need to be brought to justice if they violate the Constitution. Our morality must be upheld by our elected officials. A nation cannot function without an understanding of right and wrong.

One difference between my generation and my son's is that of morality. Many from my generation are dumbfounded with all the lowering of thresholds for morality that has happened since I was a young man. But for the next generation, that of my son's, they have less of an issue with it. They grew up with scandals (Iran Contra, Whitewater, and of course the famous Lewinski case of a sitting president) and poor role models from elected officials to Hollywood and rockstar behaviors. There have been drastic changes since the 1960s, when television could not show married couples in their bedrooms, unless they were featured in separate twin beds.

The difference in society, even between the administration of Bill Clinton and that of President Barack Obama, has reached more complacency and a greater acceptance of immorality. Former President Clinton once admitted trying marijuana, stating, "But, I did not inhale." When President Obama was campaigning, he described a period in his early college years as a time that he soul-searched and did drugs. It is easy to see in these two examples that the American society did not challenge, but accepted this immorality. The public had outcry about Clinton's use of marijuana; but by the time President Obama stated his drug use, no one seemed to care about their president doing drugs.

Good morality is closely linked with influence of religion. Liberals are quick to say and believe that religion hovers more on the conservative right in our society. Religion has always been conservative in its teachings. Preservation, moderation, love and respect are all doctrines of religion. Even Mother Nature is conservative. But religion does not seem to have a position at the forefront with liberals. In response to the belief of many leftists that religion is orientated only to the right, is probably because of the reaction by religions to being undermined by the solidification of liberalism in our society. Religion is a counter-reaction to the more carefree approach to morality we see in today's liberal world. George Washington stated, "Reason and experience both forbid us to expect that national morality can prevail in exclusion of religious principles", and, "There is but one straight course, and that is to seek truth and pursue it steadily."

In his book entitled, "Our Endangered Values"[4] by former President Jimmy Carter, after pointing out how displeased he was with our current society and its moral values, blamed it all on conservatives and the Religious Right. The Religious Right has always tried to maintain high moral ground. It is what they are about. What was baffling in his book is that former President Carter was very coy the few times he mentioned Bill Clinton. With the Clinton/Lewinski case so prevalent, it is surprising that the author blamed only conservatives and the Religious Right, specifically, for the lack of morality. Bill Clinton put morality at its lowest point during his presidency.

This shocked me that someone who led our country for four years is unable to see the liberal society we are immersed in and reinforces my observation that liberals do not know when they are deep into liberalism. School shootings and the disrespect we have for our educators should be proof enough. Parents run to lawyers, instead of reinforcing educators when there is an issue with their child at school. This is what a liberal society causes. Liberals do not know when it is time to draw the line and return to center. This unfortunately, puts them deeper and deeper into socialistic principles.

Some infamous examples of immorality are the affairs of the Kennedys, and Senator Gary Hart (mentioned earlier). Hart was considered the Democrat front runner for the 1988 election, but he was caught by the media in the Caribbean with a young woman, while his wife was back on the continent. More recently, there was the John Edwards affair, just after his 2008 Democrat run for nomination. Also in 2008, the long term Republican senator from Idaho, Larry Craig, was caught by an undercover police officer when the senator played footsie with the officer in an airport bathroom. That same year, another long term senator Ted Stevens from Alaska, was cited for accepting gifts and free home renovations. Then in 2009, a state governor tried to hide his affair by saying he was hiking the Appalachian Trail, when he was actually in South America visiting his girlfriend. The list goes on. We need to get back to where morality controls our government and society, not just freespirited hypocrites.

Ironically, it seems most of these Democrats accused of an injustice are able to remain in office, while the Republicans do not. I think it is the morality of the right that puts pressure on them. Our founding fathers warned about removing religion and morality from government, that it would result in tyranny. Thomas Jefferson addressed this, "God who gave us life gave us liberty. And can the liberties of a nation be thought secure if we have removed their only firm basis: a conviction in the minds of men that these liberties are the gift of God? That they are not to be violated but with His wrath?"

- **TERRORIST ORGANIZATIONS.** We must protect our borders and maintain a ready military. We need to purge our society from ideological brainwashing that certain groups do to our young impressionable students, who have not yet enough life knowledge to make their own decisions.

We need to do a real war declaration against terrorist organizations. This will bring about war-time legislation and policies. This is ultimately the only way we are going to rid ourselves of this nuisance. Once these terrorists have obtained enough fissionable material to build atomic bombs, it will be too late to correct our unpreparedness. We need to keep our military prepared. Hand-in-hand with protecting our great nation, we need to protect our borders. If citizens of a border nation (such as Mexico) wish to risk everything to come to our nation, we need to work with those countries to solve the reason(s) why they wish to leave so badly.

- **SINGLE RACE ORGANIZATIONS AND MERIT SYSTEM.** We must all strive first to be Americans. Attention should not be given to one group over another, and the last of the separatist racial organizations should be eliminated. Do not make emphasis of one group over the other. Devoting a full month to any one race, group, or religion is not fair to all others in this collective society.

  We need to also maintain a national sovereignty without a national second language. Strength comes from uniformity and solidarity. All groups now in America have the same opportunities and protection under the law. We need to return to merit systems, our individual abilities are what should be recognized.

  Single race orientated organizations should be disbanded. If we are all Americans we only need one all inclusive beauty pageant. Single race, or organizations based on color or ethnicity are in themselves racist. Those organizations only concentrate on one group, which is racial and anti-American to all other groups.

- **HISTORY SHOULD NEVER BE CHANGED.** It is a fact, that the person who made the most documented discovery of America was Christopher Columbus, even though in recent years this has been de-emphasized. We did step on the moon in 1969. The Holocaust really did occur, and six million Jews were exterminated, and 9/11 really did occur and was not a conspiracy (there was even live coverage on television and the internet). Written history should not be changed even by Hollywood. Thomas Jefferson wrote, that, "A morsel of history is a thing so rare as to be always valuable."

  At the writing of this book, the administration of Iran declared that the Holocaust was a myth and that it did not occur during World War II, and that over six million Jews were not exterminated. But, the Holocaust was witnessed by General Dwight D. Eisenhower, which prompted him to say the following, "Those who cannot remember [or believe] the past, are condemned to repeat it." Because he wanted a documented history of the Holocaust, General Eisenhower collected as much as he could in photographs, films, and testimonials. When faced with the results of the Holocaust first hand, he stated, "The day will come when some 'son of a bitch' will say that this never happened."

Unfortunately, history repeats itself. People quickly forget, and then after a time go into denial. It was not long after 9/11 that you began to hear conspiracy theories.

In conclusion, most people find politics boring, but it is crucial that everyone be familiar with politics, government, and those that we elect to make decisions for us. The judicial system has long acknowledged that ignorance of the law is no excuse. Citizens need to extend this to everyday politics and government as well.

Many people ride the tide until changes upset their status quo, or until a disaster (whether natural, social, or political) occurs that affects their lives, family, or community. People generally think in smaller spheres and in basic social patterns. We want to be comfortable, just as our neighbors, relatives, and friends do. People just want to live peacefully and raise their children. Our primeval needs are simple.

"Those who choose to sacrifice freedom in order to gain security shall not have, nor do they deserve, either one."   ~ Benjamin Franklin

CHAPTER SEVEN
ELECTIBILITY

Newly Elected Official
Do what you may in hopes to improve. Change what you can, but don't lose track of the common citizen. It is still their wishes you must heed, their whims and cycles you must know, their social mores you must keep; they are who elected you.
                                                                    ~ The Author

Americans are well trained. During an election we voice our candor and emotions. Then, after elections, we go about our business in a robotic complacency. When it comes to voting, many voters are like naïve consumers. They feel alienated and do not believe their one vote will make any difference. I find a good portion of Americans are weak on ideology; too trusting and complacent about their government, and function usually with the here and now. Most do not have the interest to keep up on all these issues. Most people just live their lives and put up with the annoyances of government. As changes in administration, policy, and taxes occur, they pay the increases and try to make ends meet as best as possible. Politics can be intense and requires much upkeep in following new bills in Congress, changes, laws, etc. Apathy, naïvety, and economic ignorance are a few reasons why the voting public does not make wise voting decisions. In a constitutional republic, the true description of the United States of America, where each vote is important, those who do not maintain a good knowledge of events and trends are unfair to the rest of us in their vote.

As human beings we are all creatures of habit. We all fall into error. It is easy for us to become apathetic. In addition most voters are unaware of the facts, issues, and potential costs or outcomes, and are usually overshadowed by the rhetoric, promises, and smoke screen of elections. They do not look beyond the entitlements they are enticed with. People also tend to believe the negative. Thus, during campaigns you will hear negative advertising and statements between candidates. It was Adolf Hitler that said, "The bigger the lie, the more people will believe it." Joseph Goebbels, Hitler's Minister of Propaganda, once said, "I could make a triangle into a square if I repeat it enough." We can be sure of two things: there will always be a silent majority that will hover within central parameters (mean-to-mean on the bell chart), and this group will remain complacent as they have throughout history, reacting only when the Gestapo knocks on their door. This was witnessed at the writing of this book as socialized healthcare was hurriedly legislated by the Obama Administration, with little time given to legislators to even read the bills.

Politicians are the only people in the world who create problems and then campaign against them. Candidates continuously promise things that are going to have to come out of the federal budget, which is supported by taxpayers. When watching a candidate or politician, be aware that over 90 percent of communication is through body language. Politicians have to be salespeople, and they become quite good at it. Watch politicians carefully, and listen carefully. Verify data before drawing conclusions. Stay abreast on issues. Candidates that are either far left or far right in their political ideology will not be effective at representing the masses, since their views do not reflect the greater majority of the population. If we as citizens allow it, without our input, it will happen. We allowed NAFTA to happen which sent jobs out of the country. Then we watched a president start a two-front war, and at the writing of this book, we allowed another president to create massive federal deficits, never before seen in history – indenturing future generations – literally tying the hands of our children and grandchildren, and their children. Politics is a hypocritical art, politicians lie, but data does not. If you never lie, you never have to remember anything.

We have elected officials that take their responsibility to their constituents for granted. They abuse the power in their position and the anesthetized populous allow it to happen, without the traditional consequences to the elected person's credibility and moral character. There is apathy in today's world. Many voters feel powerless to change anything or make a difference. Many are absorbed by the political rhetoric and buy into the hype. It sounds harsh, but the best way to describe this is by relating it to the family dog. The family pet is docile, willing to please, does not wish to make waves or displease, and follows the flow – but needs a master. In a similar way, many constituents also need direction.

There are many idiosyncrasies with the voting public. Since the first Catholic president, John F. Kennedy, Catholics have voted strongly Democrat, even though they believe in pro-life. Jews, as a group, tend to vote predominantly as liberal Democrats. With the unending growth of liberalism in our society, those that have attained great wealth do not necessarily feel compelled to vote conservative. It has become the "in-thing" to vote liberal. As a group, African-Americans have traditionally voted strongly Democrat, and educators stoically vote Democrat.

As we know, liberals are sensitive beyond the norm, and have a belief in socialistic equality. They think in terms of group identity, not individual identity. They speak of the *less fortunate*, the *working poor*, the *uneducated,* etc. When you think in terms of groups it is easier to organize and coordinate numbers. You do not have to deal with the independent nature of the individual. Therefore, conservatives are politically disadvantaged in this respect. Democrats are very vocal with emotions to match, and willing to redistribute wealth (tax those that have done well and give it to the poor). This is not an equitable situation to those who have taken the initiative and worked hard to build a modest life. Who would not be motivated to vote for a party that promises this gifting with little commitment to pay it back? Today, because of this, better than ninety percent of immigrants vote Democrat.

Many individual citizens become Democrat, or follow the Democrat political platform because they lack direction within themselves, and look to a party they conceive who will take care of their needs and give them direction. Others, such as educators, usually vote Democrat even though many political conservative administrations have been very favorable to education (for example the administration of George W. Bush), because they feel education will receive more benefit in tax payer dollars. Many persons, once they accumulate assets may also change their political direction because of less taxation on their nest-eggs. Others who have been staunch supporters of unions during their working life, denounce unionism once they retire. During wars and times of national concern, the electorate tends to keep the incumbent in office.

In elections Democrats always promote their platform as the party of change. What really is meant by this is that they want to be in power. They want to be elected. During elections, it is easy for Democrats to play the moderate game to draw in more votes, until elected. Then their standard political platform is imposed. Once in office, they institute their age old political agenda; increase taxes, increase social programs, increase the size of government, reduce the military, etc. Once in power, level-headed moderate Democrats get overshadowed by their more liberal and vocal counterparts; and therefore, the liberal faction sets the direction. Even with all the rhetoric that President Obama presented about working with both sides, and that he was the change that would set a new direction, the liberal faction took precedence, especially in their long-awaited earmarks, which were readily put into President Obama's stimulus packages.

Liberals may use limited or distorted data or statistics to support a claim that in many cases has not been rationalized to its full extent. In many party platform issues they suffer the unintended consequences of their actions. A good example is their ongoing platform to tax higher wage earners and businesses, while promising to their constituents (the lesser wage earners) that they will be the benefactor. What really happens is that businesses, in order to survive, raise prices and pass the increased taxes on to the consumer thus, making the increase come full circle to everyone. Imagine the increases in groceries, fuel for automobiles and home, electricity, clothing; all consumer goods. What is also not rationalized is that tax increases cause a slowing of consumer purchasing, therefore, less revenue for businesses, which equates into a loss of taxes for the government. Their promises, even though well meant, because of not rationalizing the full extent and effects of the tax increases, totally defeats their purpose. This happens again and again.

Do not trust a "smooth" candidate. But the populous will vote for them each time. What we have is a dilemma. Because of the characteristics of the Promoter Personality discussed earlier, a person of that style should not be in high elected positions. But the fact of the matter is, just like a salesman in a corporation, they are able to talk and maneuver themselves into such positions easier than the other Personality Styles because of their natural communicative abilities, energy, and quest for power and limelight. Another reason this Personality Style is drawn to politics is that Promoters love abstract reasoning, not the nuts-and-bolts of the sciences, or the detail necessary to analyze a spreadsheet.

In elections, the silent majority actually gets quelled by the overt and squeaky wheel of the Promoter Personality. There are many things the potential electorate does not consider when they follow the left. They support the Democrat Party only because it is supposed to be "The party of the people." But many of their overt and underlying liberal hypocrisies sooner or later may push many away. It is easy to fall into the liberals' hype, sensitivities, and insecurities. They just connect better. Each of us needs to be a better judge of character, and keep ourselves educated on the candidates, issues and events that surround us.

President Harry Truman and former Vice President Walter Mondale, under Jimmy Carter, were the last honest Democrats of the twentieth century. Not based on their policies but their honesty and integrity. Mondale would have been the first president from Minnesota, had he won the 1984 election. During his Democrat Party acceptance speech, one of the many things he said was, "You know we will have to raise taxes." He was honest enough to admit it, right during his acceptance speech to all the delegates present. I respected him for doing it, but at the same time I said to my wife, who was watching the speech with me, that he just lost the election! He was not elected. I doubt the Democratic National Committee will allow such rhetoric anymore at their national conference.

Who would be the best candidate for president? It should be someone with a diverse background of experiences. A person, who has spent some time in the military, has traveled extensively, has had experience in business and government, is married and has children. This would help make a well-rounded candidate, one who would make decisions based on all their experiences, all parts of our culture and directions -- and preferably not of the Promoter Personality Style. It does not mean much for liberal voters if a candidate has military experience, but military experience is a good sign of leadership and bearing in an elected representative. We would like a superhero to lead us. A person with as few faults and background influences as possible. No one is perfect, but we, as the voting public expect near perfect characteristics. Minimally the candidate should possess good judgment and know when to be decisive, and when to compromise, he or she must be honest and upstanding, have dignity and bearing.

A President must be a good decision maker, be fair and just, and morally responsible. They must lead in a nuclear and terrorist age. Not all persons can successfully step up to the plate. And no matter the time in history, or the issues, citizens should never consider voting for a candidate that does not have good credentials, especially if they are unwilling to share them with the voters. If a candidate for president does not want to share their natural birth certificate, their college thesis and academic work, records pertaining to their private sector experience, or their military history, then they should not be allowed to represent the citizens of the United States. The vetting process for all potential candidates needs to be thorough. Thomas Jefferson wrote, "No man will ever bring out of the Presidency the reputation which carries him into it."

America has not been gifted with wholesome presidents in recent decades. The Clintons came to their campaign with allegations of inappropriate affairs from multiple young women, which ultimately ended in the Monica Lewinski case. Hillary had some questionable land dealings through a former law partnership. Then George W. Bush got us into a two-front war against terrorism. And there remains skepticism in the minds of many Americans about the credentials of

Barack Obama, concerning his citizenship, lack of overall experience, and his reluctance to let us know more about him; such as what his thesis was on at Columbia, and the impact of his pre-presidential associations, such as with Reverend Wright, ACORN, and his stature in not so savory Chicago politics. "Make yourself an honest man, and then you may be sure that there is one less scoundrel in the world", wrote the Scottish writer and historian, Thomas Carlyle.

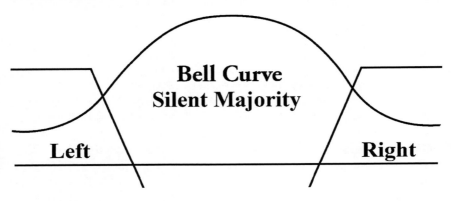

Based on the political bell chart illustrated above, how can a liberal on the far left, or someone on the far right effectively represent the masses? How can they represent their constituents and know the reality of the world when viewed from such a far liberal or conservative position? Their ideology is limited. Our presidents are the temporary stewards of this nation – their job is to uphold the constitution and fulfill the needs and requests of the American citizen. Too many presidents have forgotten this. Once in power, it becomes an egocentric fulfillment for them instead. It is not unusual to hear citizens say, "I really fear for America these days. I feel a lot of anger, disappointment and disillusionment with our government and elected officials." This concern is compounded by the budget deficits we are amassing, high unemployment, and the apathy of the voting public to elect good persons for the highest offices.

In our world there is more and more danger in electing inexperienced leaders. Selection of a candidate comes down to "buyer beware." If the candidate is a smooth talker and can captivate an audience, it only shows that he or she has good delivery, good communication skills, but do they have tangible personal leadership skills? What is their track record? These are crucial questions. Remember, elections are a numbers game. The only thing that elected officials respect and will cause them to take heed, are numbers – that is, numbers against them!

Independents and conservatives must be the voice to return America to an intelligent future. We have been put in liberal despair, and, as we have learned throughout this text, is that liberals never know when to draw the line. It must be the independents and conservatives to put this nation back on track. We need to continue to be very skeptical of our elected officials, because for decades they have not been listening to us. Instead, they have utilized their position and power for their own means and agendas.

CHAPTER EIGHT

HOW WE CAN TELL WE ARE IN A LIBERAL SOCIETY

Your first indication that we are in a liberal society is that devout liberals are relatively happy. They are a very vocal part of society, especially when they feel wronged, or when society is moving to the right. Therefore, if these devout liberals are generally satisfied with the status quo society, and complain or blame less, it is a good indicator we are in a liberal society.

The following are indications of the left-of-center era we are in:

- **THE BELIEF THAT GOVERNMENT WILL SOLVE ALL CONCERNS OF THE MASSES.** A liberal society expands government, which has to be paid for by more taxes. Taxes are increased on the masses, but especially on higher income persons, businesses, corporations, and any other means of taxation is sought to maintain a larger government.

    There are more social programs than ever before, and the quest for social entitlements, like socialized medicine is dominant, with less emphasis on personal responsibility. The liberal government always attacks higher wage earners and business to fund these programs with little concern how it will affect these entities. Therefore, liberalism expands government which has to be paid for by individual taxes. The government then redistributes these taxes. Again, the government is the greatest Ponzi scheme ever.

    So strongly do liberals believe in government that the following comment was made during the time of this writing by a Minnesota state Democrat Senate Majority Leader: "I believe that it is simplistic and naïve to assume that taxpayers can spend their money better than the government." What is shocking is that this statement comes from someone who has studied economics at a university. Thomas Jefferson stated that, "Government is best which governs the least, because its people discipline themselves."

- **EVERYTHING HAS BECOME POLITICALLY CORRECT AND OVERLY SENSITIVE.** Telling of jokes has been eliminated in society. Sensitivity training becomes the norm. Political correctness causes complications and fear of being wrong. Political correctness dumbs down America. Society and government has gotten very polarized (liberal verse conservative).

121

With oversensitivity, anything remotely suggesting any unpleasantness or jeopardizing to any group, regardless how it will affect the mass majority and erode personal wealth and responsibility, is frowned upon and not practiced. Example: profiling to help law enforcement to operate more effectively, or to protect national security. It has been mentioned that liberal candidates in Minnesota considered it too insensitive to put tags on license plates to denote a foreign national. Even with the threat of declared war to America by terrorists they resisted this. With liberals there is less and less of a clear line between right and wrong, and between constructive sensitivity and overt sensitivity gone awry. Hypocrisy thrives on the left.

The political left tolerates a lot in the name of humanity. But they do not seem to have a balance, or know when enough is enough, or a rational end to their sensitivity. In many instances they oversensitize and in so doing create other problems. Such as their reluctance to move beyond the plight of the illegal immigrant, instead they treat them like citizens and vote to give them social security. More shocking, is giving Miranda rights to terrorists and enemies of our society in the name of liberalism, as instituted by President Barack Obama. A liberal society does not dwell on anything negative. To them, the world is just one big happy place.

Without order (the courts, law enforcement, civil rights and constitutions) and religion, a society will quickly go into chaos and people will quickly return to basic survival mode, obtaining their needs, by any means they feel necessary.

- **LESS FORMALITY IN SOCIETY, EVERYTHING IS CASUAL.**
  We have lost our formality in dress and etiquette. This in its way is not respecting those institutions, festivities, people and traditions that give us our dignity. Teachers no longer dress the part of their position, and have lost respect from their students. Many remember when school clothes and play clothes became the same. Before, when a child got home from school each day, he would have to change into his play clothes before he did anything else.

- **THE YOUNGER GENERATION IS OFFSETTING THE DOMINANCE IN LIBERALISM BY DRIFTING MORE TO THE MIDDLE AND CONSERVATIVE SIDE.** Conservatives are becoming more disillusioned, more vocal and upset by the political and social trends. Many individuals, groups, and organizations are taking initiative, and use their own budgets to promote solutions for society, because congress is not listening to the people. During the 2008 elections this was obvious when Mr. T. Boone Pickens proposed an energy strategy for the nation with his own funds. He promoted his ideas on national media. Taxes, energy costs, terrorism, and economy have all taken a toll on the populous, which has manifested into an all time low approval rating of Congress. Because of this inability to see the problems and try to solve them, Congress has a very low approval rating.

- **SPECIAL EMPHASIS, COVERAGE, AND SUPPORT OF A DEMOCRAT PRESIDENT AND ELECTED OFFICIALS, ESPECIALLY DURING AN ELECTION YEAR. THE MEDIA, AS ALREADY DISCUSSED, IS CORRUPT WITH LIBERALISM.** To learn both sides of issues you must go to conservative stations so you can learn what is not broadcast by the dominant liberal media. Example: during the Iraq war, under the Bush Administration, even though it was not popular, and questionable at the time if the US needed to intervene into Iraq, none of the positive events (free elections, lifting of Saddam Hussein's iron hand, ethnic cleansing, discovery of mass graves, etc.), were mentioned, or at best, downplayed by the bias media. This changed after President Obama inherited the war. With typical hypocrisy, the media was then more willing to report the positive events.

The media is dominated by the liberal left, and is doing a disservice because it refuses to report both sides of issues, and in the case of conservative action, such as the events in Iraq, the goodwill was never reported. I had to rely on a Colonel who returned from Iraq with a 75 minute DVD about the good things happening in Iraq. This arrogance of the media is censorship to the American public, and should be considered at the very least poor ethics and a disservice to Americans.

As I have mentioned, a Democrat president is treated preferentially by the media as compared to a Republican president. This double standard is easily seen on the evening news and in daily newspapers.

- **A HEIGHTENED CONCERN FOR THE ENVIRONMENT, EVEN AT THE DISADVANTAGE TO THE ECONOMY.** There are increased proposals for government money to fund environmental programs. There is an overall increased consciousness on the environmental subject, regardless of the need for a balance of environment and economy. This is another hypocrisy of the liberal. The liberal does not want to put many restrictions on immigration or government expenses, but at the same time will not utilize our natural resources to offset the growing population and need for expanded energy.

- **THERE IS AN OVERALL SOCIAL APATHY, LACK OF INDIVIDUAL CONCERN AND ACCEPTANCE OF NEGATIVE SOCIAL AND MORAL ACTIONS AND BEHAVIORS OF PERSONS IN OUR CULTURE.**
This is especially true with those in the Democratic Party and the entertainment industry. This was quite evident with the tolerance given to the Clinton/Lewinski affair and the poor credentials of Barrack Obama as a presidential candidate (who also had questionable American affiliations).

Following this liberal trend is the new leniency on immigration. Restrictions on aliens (non-citizens), including illegal aliens are relaxed. This shows the slow reluctance of the left to address the illegal immigration problem. It was obvious with the 2008 resolution that gave illegal aliens social security in an age when many of our own children were struggling to find jobs and are not sure if they will receive social security in their future.

Traditional organizations like the Boy Scouts, Girl Scouts, and other such traditional groups have greatly reduced memberships and presence in our society.

- **THE CRIMINAL JUSTICE SYSTEM IS SOFT ON CRIME.**
Crime is viewed not from the aspect of the victim so much as from empathy of the rudimentary social cause of crime. Example: "Sure he did a bad thing, but he grew up in the ghetto and had a poor childhood with only one parent." This sensitivity of the political left has been described as, "A soft-hearted and soft-headed approach to crime." The old expression holds true, "If you do the crime, you will do the time."

People have said today's prisons are too nice -- there is less incentive to stay out of them. You hear, "Three hots and a cot." Prison is no longer a real deterrent, unlike when chain gangs did improvement for society in the early 20th century, such as road construction and maintenance. The concept was that this would help work off their debt to society. I do not propose a return to the same treatment of the era, but think it would be good for prisoners to pay back society for their abuses of it, this may instill a better perspective of right and wrong for them.

Crime escalates with less guidance and compliance from parents, society, individuals, institutions, and our education system. It has forced the criminal justice system to compensate through "get tougher" sentencing and less tolerant policies. This attests to the statement, "A soft judge creates hardened criminals." It is interesting in today's world to observe persons charged. While showing their arrest, or while walking to and from court trials or a detention center, they no longer cover their heads in embarrassment. They no longer seem embarrassed by their acts against society and its citizens. In past decades you saw remorse in those arrested when they tried to shield their face from the media and local citizens, in an admission that they failed society and our cultural morals. Those in a socialized society do not appear to have the remorse, only the realization that they got caught.

- **THE MILITARY IS DRASTICALLY REDUCED, LEAVING A DELAY IN RECRUITMENT OF MILITARY PERSONAL AND MATERIAL FOR ANY NATIONAL OR LOCAL EMERGENCY.**
We live in a world which increasingly seems to be shrinking because of the use of technology and globalization, which also allows for more terrorist groups to infiltrate our society. In world politics it comes down to peace through strength and readiness. George Washington warned: "If we are wise [as a nation], let us prepare for the worst."

President Clinton during his term had drastically reduced the military; therefore America was not fully prepared for the terrorism that occurred on September 11, 2001. Reduction of military budget is an ongoing platform with Democrats; then conservatives come into office and have to re-establish the budget to maintain readiness.

- **GROWTH OF CONSERVATIVE TALK RADIO STATIONS TO OFFSET THE EXISTING LIBERAL SOCIETY.**
There is a marked increase in conservative authors and publications trying to offset the leftist society. Society always tries to neutralize itself. Talk radio listeners are also searching for more information and balance that they do not receive from the mainstream media.

In today's world there are more conservative stations than liberal based stations. This is because, first, listening to liberal stations is not that easy. There is a lot of hype, emotion and repetition of liberal concerns, with less emphasis on detail. Whereas the many conservative stations supply plenty of detail, analysis and, in some cases, almost beat a subject to death in their discussion of it. Secondly, liberals do not like data and do not do well with a lot of statistics. They would be overwhelmed by listeners phoning in with data and opinions. The many conservative stations are an outcome of, and an offset, to the predominant liberal society. Liberals tend to listen to *National Public Radio (NPR)*.

My experience with tuning in on conservative talk radio stations is that they are visited almost daily by the left. Some reasons for this is that conservative talk radio obtains more diverse information of the subject, or issue, and second, liberals listen and call in to defend the liberal side of an issue. Radio is only an auditory medium. Promoters like action, sensationalism and hype. This explains why there are many television stations that function more at the liberal end. Televised media has truly become a business which deflects credibility by instilling fear, sensationalism, and hype -- anything to drive ratings. In an attempt to be a liberal counterpart to talk radio, *Air America* only lasted several years.

The first time I remember seeing any emotion by a news reporter was Walter Cronkite, when he announced the assassination of John F. Kennedy. After the announcement, he took his glasses off and wept as the camera continued to roll.

- **LACK OF DISCIPLINE IN OUR SCHOOLS HAS LED TO EVENTS NEVER BEFORE OCCURRING IN OUR PUBLIC EDUCATION.** Educators are powerless with the use of discipline. We have to rely on our local police, more than ever before, in our schools as a replacement for the respect our educators once received. Educators turn to the police; and parents, their lawyers when a discipline issue comes up in school.

As a child, when I was attending public school, if I got into trouble, I would get into trouble again at home, with some form of discipline bestowed upon me for not behaving in school. Those were the days that parents supported the schools and educators -- and there were no school shootings! The liberal polarization that has been controlling society for the past decades has eliminated discipline in schools and in its place, has created the environment for school shootings.

Unbelieving to the reader is the fact that on occasion when I was in high school, friends would sometimes bring a gun to school for trade. We would stand by a locker and examine the potential purchase. This was not unusual to see during those years. But we never used the guns we brought to school. We only brought them there to buy or sell. Our Christian moral upbringing with love of God and country would not have allowed us to go down the emotional road to a school shooting.

Decades of liberal ideology, politics, and good economy helped create the *Millennium Generation*, considered to be those persons born between 1982 and 1999. That generation of our offspring born into a world of excesses, dual family incomes, the world at their keyboard, few needs and wants, and a society where you do not take individual responsibility, but expect the government to give you your needs. They have no history of what it was like to live in a society that their pioneer relatives did, where you had self-pride, and relied on yourself, and hard work to get ahead.

Unfortunately this liberal societal abyss has caused the next generation to be very self-centered and not as loyal to companies and institutions as was the previous generation. That is why I have included in this writing a history of how our society used to be decades ago. Hopefully this will give insight and a respect for what has been and how America used to function (See, Chapter Eleven, "Changes Since I Was A Child").

WHY ARE COLLEGES AND UNIVERSITIES AND THEIR FACILITY PREDOMINANTLY LIBERAL?

There has always been a liberal focus on college campuses, albeit not as much as it has gained in the last four decades. There has always been a *conformity of non-conformity* among college teaching staff. What is meant by this, is college professors and teaching staff have always tried to distinguish themselves differently. It is like the Promoter Personality exercising its freedom by being different. In my early days of college, professors used to grow their hair long until it became the custom of my generation to have long hair. The stereotypical bow-tie used to be another symbol that has been used, as was the corduroy jacket. The list goes on depending on the era of which you are speaking. Just as fads develop and dissipate or change, iconic fads of college professors also change with time. They try to look different and express themselves differently. This comes from their liberal belief to express choices and freedoms since colleges and universities promote free expression and thought.

Colleges and universities to some degree have always allowed free thinking. It is considered part of the learning process. Four decades ago more people started going to college. This was prompted by a quest for more knowledge, military deferments during an unpopular war, and something to do while deciding what to do in your life. This was a changing time in America. A great majority of young people were questioning their government, personal liberties, and experimenting with mind altering drugs, such as LSD. To counter-balance the conservative society, which the previous generation was born into and adopted, there was a turn toward liberalism. This happened to the greatest degree on college campuses, and has continued today. Persons who were young liberals and entered college in the 1960s and 1970s, have entrenched themselves in college tenure and are now the liberal status quo of higher academia. It is almost certain that this liberal trend in higher education will continue, but hopefully be more counterbalanced with future generations. It appears a natural event, that leftists are drawn to academia and politics.

It is true, that in colleges and universities in America, liberals outnumber conservatives two to one.[1] This ratio increases in liberal arts (no pun intended!) and social sciences. Conservatives tend to go into business, accounting, finance, and economics to be successful in the private sector and make money, so they will ultimately have a comfortable life. Conservatives are practical, they want to know how to do things, what will ultimately benefit, or work for them and give a payback; while liberals are more abstract in their reasoning. Academia gives the liberal wide parameters and autonomy, which fits well ideologically into the idiosyncratic needs of the liberal psyche.

Another reason why liberalism reigns on campuses across the nation is that many of the persons that are drawn to this livelihood are already of an independent, liberal mind. For many professors, a good portion of their life has been immersed in academia and bureaucracy. Their experience outside of these institutions (such as the free market, private sector), has been very limited. Therefore, they adhere to what they are most familiar with. They grew up going to school, graduated and went to college, obtained a higher degree, and then begin teaching at a college. Thus, it is speculative what experience they have gained outside the walls of academia.

Professors as a group are also liberal because they have a disdain for capitalism. This may play into their insecurities with power and envy and therefore, liberal professors see forms of socialism as an antagonist to capitalism. Liberals believe capitalism to be unjust because it does not have uniformity and equality that a socialist system would give. Capitalism rewards those with ambition, persistence, self-reliance and taking risk. In a capitalist system, a risk taking, motivated entrepreneur can do well and make a lot of money. There is no short-cut to riches; you must work hard, prepare yourself through education and experience, and stay educated to trends and changes. You must be ready to act when trends and markets alter.

For those who have not wished to prepare themselves, have made poor decisions, those who just don't have the desire or drive for entrepreneurship, or have struggled with substance abuse; there are provisions in capitalism to maintain those persons with a basic living and quality of life. This is done through social welfare and assistance programs to get those persons back on their feet. Capitalism always rewards hard work.

It is important to point out that many people may go into business, but many do not survive the traditional three to five years it may take to break even. Obviously, this was not the risk or uncertainty the professor wished to undertake in his life. But, if we did not have entrepreneurs who take risks, who try again when they fail, we would not have small, medium, or large businesses and corporations hiring the populous and paying the majority of revenues to our government in taxes. If anything, the capitalist should be revered by liberals, because the capitalist takes the initiative, works hard, persists over failures, and in so doing, builds our economy. Without the entrepreneur our society would implode upon itself.

Teachers or professors cannot escape the principles of capitalism or free market philosophies even in their college or university setting. They must please their clients (students) by supplying a good product and service. Professors must gear toward their client's psyche, needs, and wishes (marketing), to prove their worth and viability, just as a salesperson caters to the idiosyncrasies of their clients. In the case of college-age students, many are still adherent to an adolescent mindset. At their young stage of life they are usually idealistic and liberally orientated. Lastly, liberal government is also perceived to be more open to support of such institutions of higher learning; therefore, those in academia have sensitivities to the Democrat Party.

Our young need to graduate from public education and college having received a good character education. They should be nurtured throughout their learning to love America and know what it stands for instead of angry with America. They should be given the tools to be good citizens. Colleges and universities and their teaching staffs should uphold this standard. To enter real life and be successful, students must unlearn many of the ideological myths promoted in our liberalized education system.

CHAPTER NINE

WHY A PREDOMINANT THIRD PARTY?

If your actions inspire others to dream more, learn more, do more, and become more, you are a great leader.
~ *John Quincy Adams*

If our voice is taken, then dumb and silent we will be led to slaughter.
~ *George Washington*

During the writing of this book, various sources reported as high as 35-40 percent of the electorate consider themselves as independents or undeclared. Other polls found that about twenty percent of the polled population consider themselves liberal. The remainder of the populous considers themself moderate or conservative. Polling usually has a three to five percent error rate, and this will vary from week to week, or month to month, especially if there is an active campaign going on. A poll in 2008, found that 38 percent of the polled population considered the current political climate too far to the left; by 2009 the same poll showed that 46 percent of those polled felt the United States was too far to the left.

The old saying, "Figures don't lie, but liars sure figure" holds especially true for politicians. The truth is, all politicians lie. They lie to get elected, for them this is business as usual. So why are citizens surprised when politicians lie after they are elected? Politicians dress things up and play with data and figures, this is also their approach to legislation. That is why this book stresses term limits for all elected politicians. Term limits will keep good rotation of politicians; and therefore, new ideas and innovation, not the amassing of unwarranted power. I have always been mystified by how those elected to federal positions seem to have great personal wealth after only a few short years in office. Elected positions were never meant to become a way of life. The growth of Libertarian and Tea Party movements have developed because people are unhappy with the current political environment and want balance.

An independent middle party would give another choice to America, and would blend issues. The growing movement toward the middle is an outcome of the dissatisfaction Americans have with our government and society as it is today. We have hovered to the left of center in our social and political base.

Liberalism has been the smog that has polluted our society for the last four decades, and has been eating away at our culture. As a populous, we have accepted two main political poles since the early beginnings of our nation. We need more choices, more options, more ideas and direction. Our culture is demanding more solutions. We are not getting quality in our government, in elected officials, and in those who run for president. Remember: If you concentrate your ideology on the far left, or the far right, you begin to suffer intolerance. The farther to the left or right you go, the more intolerant you become.

Throughout political history there have been many independent parties that have evolved and disintegrated. Over the past they have been an important part of the political mix. At times, independent political parties have captured as much as sixteen percent of the popular vote. Usually these parties have taken votes from either the Democrat or Republican base, and therefore have affected elections in one direction or the other. The two-party system evolved during the 1850s. The two dominant political parties in America, Democrat and Republican, win the majority of federal, state, and local elections. Independent parties have usually evolved because of a particular ideology, an important issue of the day, or the ideology or charisma of a particular candidate. Many independent parties have been splinter groups from the two major parties and have drawn individuals from the dominant party. This has obviously given the opposing party an advantage in votes.

Several independent parties were formed prior to the Civil War on issues relating to slavery. The Prohibition Party was formed in 1869 as a single issue party to abolish the sale and consumption of alcohol. The Progressive Party (also called Bull Moose Party) was formed in 1912 and nominated former president Theodore Roosevelt as its candidate, but Woodrow Wilson (Democrat) was elected. In 1924 an independent party called the "League for Progressive Political Action" was supported by Robert M. La Follette (D–WI).[1] The party received sixteen percent of the popular vote, but Calvin Coolidge (Republican) won the election. In more recent history, H. Ross Perot, a Texas businessman, ran as an independent in the 1992 and 1996 campaigns. In the 1992 election he received ninteen million votes.

Ever since we have had a two-party system independent parties have come and gone based on the issues of the day. But no independent party has ever won a national election. They have only influenced the outcome of national elections because they drew voters away from the established parties. If the independent party drew from the Democrats, the likelihood was that the Republican candidate would win, and vice-versa. The American voter has not accepted a dominant, third national party. Other nations have a variety of dominant parties. A good example is Mexico and other South American countries, where it is not unusual to have many predominant national parties.

Most American citizens are law abiding persons that just follow the flow of society. As long as their basic needs are met, they are content. As long as families have food, shelter, a livelihood, and community services, they are comfortable and enjoy life. All persons first live in a community, whether it is urban or rural; then a county; and next, under a representative district; then state and federal government. Generally, in our two-party system, votes are divided almost equally between Democrats and Republicans. Elections usually only vary by several percentage points, but many times is evenly divided. Therefore, whoever is elected is only favored by half the population. It is usually only one or two percent that push elections over to one side or the other. This small percent of the population are usually the more informed voters that have followed issues and current events of the day.

There is apathy among voters. They may vote for a particular candidate because of a single issue in their life, are reluctant to admit right or left status for fear of ridicule, or are swayed by the rhetoric or personality of the candidate. There are many reasons for people to vote the way they do. Few, however, are logical reasons. You may have relatives that were strongly committed to parties that supported union philosophy, but then these same relatives changed their party affiliation after they had retired and wanted to save their income from taxation. We need to approach a third party from an ideological, grass-roots perspective, so people understand from the ground up why they believe the way they do. Many people do not know anymore why they are a Democrat or a Republican. The parties have changed, and so has our society.

More than ever, our nation needs a strong third national party. Our two predominant parties are polarized, and struggle to work together. Our founders did not believe in a party system because of concerns that it would polarize the government and legislation. A strong third party will give another option to what we currently have. From the bell chart in Chapter One we see that the majority of Americans are comfortable hovering in the center politically. The middle platform gives the distinct advantage of flexibility.

In everyday life, when approached with a problem you have the option to live with it, leave it (if that is possible), or fix it. To fix a problem you can change your own behavior. To change the behavior of others is more difficult; but, that is what must be done to ultimately change the system. There is no doubt that America needs a tune-up. Surveys consistently show that a third, or better of the population, consider themselves to be independent, and this number is growing. If these citizens voted for a national middle third party leader, there is little doubt that we would have the first elected third party president.

How can a candidate effectively represent us from either of the two extremes? If they are a liberal Democrat or ultraconservative Republican, how can they be unbiased for the mass of society in the middle? We are not going to change either extreme sphere. The pressure of a third party will add the extra layer of comparison, and neutralize both spheres more than by any other means. The retaking of America and rebuilding of the individual pioneer spirit will fall on the middle of the road. Leftists will never read this book or question their own ideology. An extreme conservative may be too set in their ways to buy into it. It is up to the non-liberal moderates to move America back to center.

American politics used to meet in the middle on issues and concerns, but has, over the decades, traveled to poles. We have moved to government take-over and mandating, where federal government forces its programs on the populous. This is a major issue with the legislation of Barack Obama's Administration. We must put country before party, not issues and personal agendas before citizens. Citizens want to believe in their government and the system, and only ask that our elected servants acknowledge our wishes. Government is the umbrella that covers all.

Some Middle Party Goals

- Promote the Independent party as a viable option and an additional voice.
- Approach politics by issues, not party, and leave your left or right politics at the door.
- Protect our nation from internal and external terrorism.
- Re-evaluate federal government as to its effectiveness and efficiency in the 21st century, consider such issues as unicameral government, and questioning the effectiveness of the Electoral College.

- Maintain good moral, social, political and religious integrity, and hold violators of the public trust both socially and judicially responsible.
- Maintain English as the national and standard language.
- Initiate legislation to introduce term limits for all elected politicians, and eliminate interest groups and earmarks, and re-evaluate all legislation and regulations that have been instituted in the last 100 years to determine its continued relevance.
- Continue our awareness of the ongoing drug problem deteriorating our nation.
- Keep our economy globally competitive with a strong free market environment.

CONCERNS WITH A THIRD PARTY

In the case of a third, or middle party, critics say that any issue from a middle perspective would just be duplicated and adapted by the other two parties at either end. Therefore, what would be the effectiveness of a middle party? Some feel there is no such thing as a political moderate, that everyone and every issue is either left or right. Where the middle differs is that it does not need to polarize on these issues or its platform. The middle may pick and choose its stance on a particular issue. It does not have to be totally polarized. The two predominant parties are stalemated toward either end; therefore, the middle ground is the greatest hope. Since a majority of citizens already hover in the middle, we should believe the old adage, "If you build it, they will come."

A middle party must maintain its own identity and agenda. Members of a middle party need to be committed to issues addressed by their party and not be swayed or react to partisan direction. Some issues, because of their focus, will naturally fall to one side or the other. In all cases, a middle party perspective must keep from sliding too deep into either sphere. A middle party must always safeguard its own identity. As with any new endeavor that pulls from existing established entities, in this case, the Democrat or Republican parties, there are natural concerns about the infrastructure of a third party. An independent middle party should not be the place for disillusioned Democrats or Republicans to hang their hat and hide from issues they disagree with from their own parties.

Critics of an independent third party, or of independent voting, say that it is difficult, and some believe almost impossible, to consistently hover in a middle range. There are always two poles to every issue; therefore, political thought of middle party members must remain on a spectrum between moderate Democrat to moderate Republican on issues. Society is also a constantly moving organism, and the consensus of the populous will periodically change in degree and gravitation.

Those that share the center have better solutions than those that hover at either end of the political spectrum. Proof is the large amount of people that hover in this mid-range. We need fiscal responsibility with focus on data, research, and common sense. There will be challenges, this is certain, but those in the middle should have credible solutions. These are the very reasons why an independent third party would be viable. Most persons approach things as a centrist. There are middle parties called Centrist Parties in many other nations. It can work. We just have to alter our thinking and prejudice. People of good faith, no matter what their original party affiliation, can find common ground as a third party member.

The Electoral College stands in the way of a national third party becoming a solidly established entity. Current policies and traditions only allow for 50 percent plus-one to win an election. The Electoral College, instituted over 200 years ago, and questioned as to its viability since its inception, would have to be drastically altered, or eliminated, to allow a national third party to persist. The popular vote is what should determine all elections. Once the last barriers are removed to having a truly dominant third party, the democratic principle of multiple choice will then be realized.

Under the Electoral College system, a President and Vice President are elected by electors who pledge their electoral vote to a specific candidate, not through a direct nationwide vote. "It is possible that an elector could ignore the results of the popular vote, but that occurs very rarely."[2] "Many different proposals to alter the Presidential election process have been offered over the years, such as direct nation-wide election by the people, but none have been passed by Congress and sent to the States for ratification."..."Reference sources indicate that over the past 200 years, over 700 proposals have been introduced in Congress to reform or eliminate the Electoral College. There have been more proposals for Constitutional amendments on changing the Electoral College than on any other subject. The American Bar Association has criticized the Electoral college as 'archaic' and 'ambiguous' and its polling showed 69 percent of lawyers favored abolishing it in 1987".[2]

"By thus failing to accurately reflect the national popular will, the argument goes, the Electoral College reinforces a two-party system, discourages third-party or independent candidates, and thereby tends to restrict choices available to the electorate."[3] The Electoral College can be changed by passing a constitutional amendment, which must be voted for by two-thirds majority in both houses of Congress, and be ratified by three-quarters of the states.

Proponents of the Electoral College are quick to point out that it has survived many challenges in its 200 year history, and continues to be a viable option, but it still does not represent the popular vote, and never will. Whenever there is an intermediary, such as the Electoral College, which ultimately determines elections, it sets the stage for bias and inequality. There is no reason, with today's technology, why we cannot rely only on the popular vote. The Electoral College reinforces a two party system, and therefore discourages third party candidates, which limits choices for the citizen voter.

The dilema is how do we have three predominent parties but still be able to represent the most people? The Tea Party has been a spontaneous response to this dilema, where a center majority is represented.

In Mexico there are three predominent political parties. In elections, several parties are permitted to form a temporary coalition to nominate candidates. The coalition must give itself a name and logo. This is unique to their system, and a way that third, or lesser parties, can capture a majority. Once elected, however, the allied party does not necessarily work as a coalition in legistlation.

Voiting is compulsory (but not enforced) for all Mexican citizens from eighteen years. Elections at all levels are direct, therefore no electoral college is utilized for any election. Federal elections are organized and overseen by a separate entity, the Ferderal Electoral Institute, which is outside of the branches of political power.

To structure a dominant third party, we must learn how to make politics interesting, easier understood and more thought provoking for the masses. That is the only way we will be able to empower the silent majority in America. They must overcome their apathy and complacency, to build a strong and lasting third party that will give the people another voice from another perspective.

CHAPTER TEN

THINGS TO KNOW TO BETTER
UNDERSTAND THE WORLD

This chapter has been included for those readers still wondering, questioning, and experiencing some basic life aspects.

THE DECADES OF LIFE

Each decade of life has its characteristics. We begin at birth. During this first decade of life (0 to 9 years old) we continue to mature and balance mental and physical growth. Each decade thereafter has its challenge and glory. A child takes information in from all of their senses. They develop motor skills, language acquisition, and socialization (interaction and testing their behaviors). The second part of this first decade sees body and mind growth and development. When you are born your first decade is discovering, and in so doing, you learn.

The second decade (10 to 19 years old) is a time of continued physical and mental growth and maturity. You begin middle school during this time and high school. You advance through the grades and begin planning your future career and livelihood, to eventually go to college, a trade school, or an early working career. Many life discoveries, especially socially, occur during this decade, and you are labeled a teenager through much of it.

The third decade of your life (20 to 29 years old), involves college and career, marriage, children, first time home buyer, and establishing yourself. There is a competitive nature between you and others of your age as you compete to get ahead and prove your worth. You may make some mistakes, but usually you have the youthful energy to move on and the time to recover.

The fourth decade of your life (30 to 39 years old), involves building your career, raising a family, traveling, and enjoying gathering with others of your age. Many persons during this time start a retirement fund or program through their work, or individually. Your life is busy and you sacrifice for your family, your spouse, your job, etc. You realize your physical shape begins to change, your body fills out. In this decade women may feel that they begin to lose their figure and youth, and begin to exercise.

The fifth decade of your life (40 to 49 years old), your children may be reaching adulthood and beginning their future plans. You are just busy and let your children and family evolve around you. Many have reached the pinnacle of their career. You try to take regular vacations, see your children go to college, and seriously address retirement plans. You are an upstanding part of your community.

The sixth decade of your life (50 to 59 years old), centers on physical changes. You become more aware of your infallibility, but because of your life experience, you make fewer wrong choices. Given proper health, you are better able to do the things you have always wanted to do. Many may become grandparents at this time, and may be caregivers to elderly parents (this has been referred to as the *sandwich era* of your lifetime; you are literally sandwiched between these responsibilities). You are in serious retirement planning. Most of your children may have established themselves by this age. You try to take vacations and begin enjoying your empty nest lifestyle. You rediscover community and take a more active part in volunteering and events. The next generation begins taking over society and you feel the changes which are now in the hands of the following generation -- your children.

The seventh decade of your life (60 to 69 years old) generally involves retirement. You are eligible for social security at this time. You enjoy traveling and visiting friends, relatives, and grandchildren. You may winter in a warmer climate. You volunteer and stay active in your local community and events.

The eighth decade of your life (70 to 79 years old) is concerned with keeping yourself healthy. You are more aware of the degenerative aging of your body and you begin to rely on others more than you ever have in the past. You may be downsizing to a smaller and more maintenance free townhome or condominium. You may have young great-grandchildren. You continue to enjoy your traveling and visiting lifestyle, but have overall slowed down. Many family events are still centered around you and your home.

The ninth decade of your life (80 to 89 years old) health issues continue to be a focus in your life. Politically, you are a dedicated voter, but your age group no longer controls the day to day activity of society or politics. You are family focused on grandchildren graduating from college and having their own children. You update and organize a family history, photographs, and heirlooms, and begin to *put your house in order.*

The tenth decade of your life (90 to 99 years old) health is your greatest concern as your body continues to change. You make peace with yourself and your maker. You tend to live by the day or week, not thinking far into the future. Some days are more of a physical challenge for you than others.

There is a time in your life that you find your inner spirit and honor it. This occurs at different times with each person. With maturity you are better able to live with ambiguity. You are not so idealistic.

MEN AND WOMEN

As a child growing up in the 1950s, when Western movies were the norm, I could never understand why there had to always be a woman in them. Even in the most remote and desolate of terrains in which the movies took place, there was always a woman included in the character cast somehow. What I learned a few years later, is that it was good marketing. By always including a woman in the western drama, you not only captured the attention of the male through the movies' action, but also of women through the interaction and romance written into the drama.

Along with the shift of society beginning in the 1960s, many groups were seeking recognition and respect. Up until the 1960s, the United States had been a white-male dominated society. Most women were housewives (homemakers in today's vernacular). With the social revolution of the 1960s, the youth liberated themselves from this stereotype and existence. Women had to first prove to themselves, and then to men, that they could be more viable citizens and create more choices for themselves.

In our present culture women have reached a precedence probably never reached before in history, but divorce in America when last investigated, was still fifty percent. That means, one in every two marriages fail and end in divorce. It is interesting to note that America and Europe are some of the few cultures on Earth that in marriage the husband and wife share assets. In China, the Arab countries, and in many other cultures, they do not share assets when they marry. The wife comes into the marriage with her assets and wealth, which is taken with her if they divorce.

Some traditional cultures like the Muslims still do arranged marriages. The pressure of the culture keeps partners together, even under the *Sharia* laws of the Muslim world, which are restrictive against women.

And Muslim men can still have up to four wives, with divorce being as simple as the husband saying, "I Divorce You" three times, and it is final. In a similar fashion, Orthodox Jews still arrange marriages. With Orthodox Jews there is little divorce because the children are trained and learn from a young age how to please and share with a partner when they marry.

The family unit, the pair-bond of a man and a woman (marriage), originally developed in small tribal groups where the male was not gone for long. The man's traditional role was to protect the group, and to hunt to provide food. This traditional role has many restrictions in a modern society. We have civilized to where men must find ways to release their natural primeval aggressiveness. Many do this through sports, game hunting and other activities. While for women, society has become safer and more civilized for them to excel. An example of the traditional male-female role was seen in our culture before the 1970s, when men would go to work and bring home a paycheck. Women would manage the household. They would clean, wash, sew and mend, take care of their children, grocery shop, and prepare meals.

MEN ARE HUNTERS ~ WOMEN ARE NESTERS
There is a natural competitiveness among the genders. Women maintain their guard around men. They do not like to show weakness nor vulnerability, nor be a burden to a man. Women want acknowledgement, appreciation, and respect. What makes women different from men is their focus on maintaining household and nurturing of the next generation. This involves selecting a mate, establishing a household (nest), bearing children, and nurturing them to adulthood. These duties have not changed since primitive tribalism, and developed over millenniums through the slow process of natural evolution.

Although many things have changed in past decades, tens of thousands of years of evolution has not changed either gender in their primeval development. In times of danger and uncertainty we see an instant reversion to these primeval characteristics. They are always there, stored in our DNA.

There are obviously many different physical and mental differences between men and women. A womans heart beats faster than a mans. Women blink twice as often as men. And women have three inches more of small intestine than do men. This probably so they can be more efficient through more absorption of nutrients from food, especially when they are carrying a child. The average woman is also five inches shorter than the average man. Women are more in tune with their bodies and natural cycles, whereas men tend to overindulge and not be as attuned.

Along the same line, women are able to make more facial expressions than men because they have more facial muscles. Therefore, women are able to express a greater range of emotions and feelings by utilizing more facial expressions, especially to young children. And this in turn helps them understand their children's many facial expressions and subtle body language. Women also have a natural tendency to avoid conflict. They have a natural instinct toward safety and caution. Again, this is nature's way of making women be more cautious and careful of their environment. In keeping themselves safe, they also assure a safe environment for their children.

There is a natural attraction to the female figure given its natural sculpting by nature. The use of the "S-curve" is taught in art to add movement, dynamics, flow and excitement to a work of art or sculpture. This imaginary line flowing through art to enhance it is also utilized by nature in the hour-glass shape of the female body. The curvature adds this flow and motion enticing its interest. As a woman, a wife, and mother; every woman has a three-part balance to maintain. A woman must be a good emotional and physical partner to her husband, a nurturing mother to her children, and a pivotal multi-tasker to maintain household by utilizing good direction, support, democracy, and economy.

Much of a woman's physical design and mental demeanor were developed by nature for child bearing and rearing. First, women are more emotional than men. This helps in their sensitivity and nurturing of children, and in their partner relationship. It keeps them more in tune to others' needs and feelings. It is also the reason they can form deep emotional feelings, relationships, and caring for their family. Without this ability, the routine duties of household, rearing children, and maintaining a partnership bond would not be as stable. This emotional bond keeps woman caring for their children and partner. The strongest bond in nature is between a mother and her child. In times of crisis, women have a natural tendency to first protect their children instead of taking flight. This again is nature's way of helping to guarantee the survival of the next generation.

As mentioned earlier, many natural characteristics inherent to women directly relate to their being able to nurture the next generation, such as maintaining a natural cleanliness. This is displayed by the automatic wiping and cleaning of a child's face after eating, regular bathing of herself and child, and tidiness of household. This cleanliness helps protect the child from disease. Also, when women explain something they go through the process how it happened, they don't just tell you the bottom-line, but the events that led up to the bottom-line. This is not what an impatient adult male wants to wait for. He does not care how it led up to the bottom-line. But, this is a natural way for children to learn and understand. A child better understands when they are shown the process, the order which allowed it to occur. Men want to know the end facts, the bottom-line. During the primeval hunt they did not have time to explain the process, they had to react. Therefore, we see that men and women react differently because of the different needs that were instilled in their early existence.

Women by nature are multi-taskers, whereas men are more linear. Multi-tasking is an age old process of women, and a natural method of keeping track of many things at once. I have watched mothers visiting with other moms, while knitting, caring for their toddlers, watching the progress of the evening meal cooking on the stove, and catching the weather forecast for the next day, all this while maintaining good communication with visiting neighbors. This natural phenomenon is related primevally to the raising of children and maintaining of a multiplicity of home management. I have watched the same multi-awareness in a mother hen with a brood of ten chicks. The hen is able to keep track of each of the chicks and their needs.

However, redundant processing can be a burden for women. Always aware of what needs to be done, and not comfortable being idle, women do not always allow themselves to enjoy the good things in their life and marriage. This includes, many times, a good physical relationship with their marriage partner. A woman may want to have intimacy with her partner, but her mind is preoccupied with the washer being fixed, the many clothes yet to be washed, and the relatives coming for the weekend. These concerns foreshadow her enjoyment, relaxation and intimacy. It obviously also confuses, and upsets her marriage partner. To men, women never seem to be able to relax, they must always be getting things done, and as such, seem to nag as they consistently remind their husbands of duties they wish to have done. There is no reason these trifles of life need to upset a marriage or relationship. Mind over matter is crucial – turn the process off, put it on the back burner. Enjoy your life, your marriage, your partner, and your intimacy.

A parent once described the difference between his sons and daughters. He said, "When my sons don't get along, I throw a ball between them, it doesn't take long and it's all over. But, my daughters can go on for days and days just over a hairbrush." Another, more outspoken female parent commented about daughters, stating, "They're cute until five, then, they're a challenge. Girls are so high maintenance I would take two boys over one girl."

TWO OF THE RICHEST MEN IN THE WORLD
It is amazing to know what one person can amass within their lifetime, *if they first prepare, make wise choices, and stay with it and never give up.* Bill Gates and Warren Buffett both have amassed billions of dollars to become two of the richest people in the world.

Bill Gates is the founder of Microsoft Corporation; he has given billions to charity through his *Bill & Melinda Gates Foundation.* The philanthropic foundation gives funds in the millions, both nationally and internationally, to many kinds of charities, research institutions, health, education, agriculture, and technology. The foundation donates to a wide variety of subjects, from eradicating Malaria, to research on why students drop out of school.

Warren Buffett started learning about finances and investment at the early age of eleven years old, when he bought his first share of stock. As a child Mr. Buffet was industrious, creative, and determined. He started a small business while in high school and had bought a forty acre parcel of land before he started college. Mr. Buffet is the owner of Berkshire-Hathaway which owns 63 companies. He has also given billions to charity.

It is obvious that one can still do well in America. Those who have done well, have done so because they started early, were willing to work hard, even if it is a paper route to begin with like Mr. Buffett. Those who have done well have also taken every opportunity to read and learn, and become educated. Mr. Buffett spends a good portion of his day reading through various media and publications. For the young he suggests a common sense approach to economy and life. Save and learn about investing, set goals and keep them, understand how interest works, and limit the need for loans. He warns about the use of credit cards and the perils of debt.

Another person who has given insight to our youth is Charles J. Sykes, author of the book, "50 Rules Kids Won't Learn In School" which gives advice to our youth in 50 rules (the first eleven are reprinted):

1. *Life is not fair. Get used to it.*
2. *The real world won't care as much about your self-esteem as much as your school does. It'll expect you to accomplish something before you feel good about yourself. This may come as a shock. Usually, when inflated self-esteem meets reality, kids complain that it's not fair (See Rule 1).*
3. *Sorry, you won't make $40,000 a year right out of high school. And you won't be a vice president or have a car phone either. You may even have to wear a uniform that doesn't have a Gap label.*
4. *If you think your teacher is tough, wait 'til you get a boss. He doesn't have tenure, so he tends to be a bit edgier. When you screw up, he's not going to ask you how you feel about it.*
5. *Flipping burgers is not beneath your dignity. Your grandparents had a different word for burger flipping. They called it opportunity. They weren't embarrassed making minimum wage either.*
6. *It's not your parents' fault. If you screw up, you are responsible. This is the flip side of "It's my life", and "You're not the boss of me", and other eloquent proclamations of your generation. When you turn 18, it's on your dime.*
7. *Before you were born your parents weren't as boring as they are now. They got that way paying your bills cleaning up your room and listening to you tell them how idealistic you are.*
8. *Your school may have done away with winners and losers. Life hasn't. In some schools, they'll give you as many times as you want to get the right answer. Failing grades have been abolished and class valedictorians scrapped, lest anyone's feelings be hurt. Effort is as important as results.*
9. *Life is not divided into semesters, and you don't get summer off. They expect you to show up every day. For eight hours. And you don't get a new life every 10 weeks. It just goes on and on.*
10. *Television is not real life. Your life is not a sitcom. Your problems will not all be solved in 30 minutes, minus time for commercials. In real life, people actually have to leave the coffee shop to go to jobs.*
11. *Be nice to nerds. You may end up working for them. We all could.*

Source: Excerpted from the book "50 Rules Kids Won't Learn in School" by Charles J. Sykes (St. Martin's Press, 2007), by permission of the author and the publisher. Because of item eleven this list has been falsely attributed to Bill Gates.

In his book Mr. Sykes lists many more rules pertaining to teenage concerns. Both Bill Gates and Warren Buffett are examples of the American dream. These are people that should be examples for us, they are self made. We should not be envious of them, we need to learn from them, not ostracize them for their accomplishment. If friends or relatives have done well, be happy for them. Your support of them will come back in great dividends. If you are envious of their accomplishments, your envy will eventually consume you. Anyone in America has the potential, you just have to read, prepare yourself, learn, and ask questions, because most of these rules are not taught in school.

If you accept advice and knowledge from those who have done better in society, and you follow their advice, it will help you be more successful, sooner in life, and with fewer setbacks. Unfortunately, most youth do not readily accept this advice or utilize it. As a young person, I did not react like most of my peers; by shunning those who had done well. My peers would ridicule those of accomplishment by saying they were only self-motivated and had come by their wealth by unethical means. Coming from a poor, middle-class family with a chemically dependent father, I was bursting at the seams to get ahead. Unlike my peers, I asked questions and learned from those who had done better. In doing so, I learned about investments, the stock market, how the free market functioned, and how these older persons had made a comfortable life for themselves.

Coming from my background, I ultimately wanted to live comfortably also. This is the hope of everyone, but many go about it wrong. They denounce those who have worked hard and made a comfortable living, accusing them of having taken advantage of the system, and having no compassion for their fellow man. That simply was not true. You cannot help others unless you can first help yourself.

CHAPTER ELEVEN

CHANGES SINCE I WAS A CHILD

I was born in the decade of the 1950s. It was a time of reconstruction from World War Two. As a child I saw the first civilian use of a rudimentary computer to match personalities on the *Art Linkletter Show* on television. Satellites were also beginning to be launched into space in a race with Communist Russia (the U.S.S.R.) to be the first to explore space. I would get up early on Saturday mornings to watch the rockets take off that would launch these satellites into space. This was long before the first manned flight occurred.

I grew up playing Cowboys and Indians, with the Lone Ranger and Tonto on TV dashing over the range on his silvery white charger. There was also Roy Rogers and Hop-A-Long Cassidy. And later, designed for television, Wagon Train, The Rifleman, Bonanza, Gun Smoke and Maverick, all western based. Western movies and cowboy singers were the vogue when I was a child. When friends came over we would invariably play Cowboys and Indians, and Cops and Robbers. We would use cap-guns and shoot at each other and say, "Bang – Bang! You're dead!" The people I knew and played with from that time never misused any real guns. Boys were able to expend their energy while still children. I even remember in high school, classmates would bring real guns to school to trade. They would complete the transactions at their lockers. Walking down the hall you would witness these exchanges with nonchalance. No one was shaken about these events and no one was ever shot. Today with school shootings, pointing even a pellet gun at someone is reason for arrest.

Since my birth to the writing of this book I have seen many changes. I was the generation of the *Hippie Era* in the 1960s and 70s. Each succeeding generation since the industrial revolution, has seen many changes during their lifetime. The last several generations have seen the most change since technology has made a constant rush forward. Can you imagine that there was a time when music videos, DVD's, the internet, personal computers, email, color television, and cell phones did not exist?

I grew up with black and white television, and there was only one station available where I lived. We had to be content and just watch whatever was on the channel at the time. Our first television set was given to us by a cousin, the screen was only nine inches wide and was overwhelmed by the big wooden box it was housed in. We also had "rabbit's ears" antenna with two telescoping rods that brought in the signal. Cable was not even invented. And, as mentioned earlier, western movies and TV series dominated the airwaves.

When I was a child, people wore watches that needed to be wound. Every other day a wrist watch or nightstand clock needed to be wound. They had the characteristic "tick-tock" as the escape wheel would release from a gear tooth. It was comforting to hear the rhythmic "tick-tock" of a clock at night. A trick with small puppies when you had to leave them alone was to put a wind-up clock with them. The ticking would comfort them by emulating their mother's heartbeat. There was also usually an electric clock (ours was in the shape of a tea kettle on the kitchen wall) that all other clocks and watches were set from.

There were wash-tub wringers on washing machines which allowed you to dry clothing by pushing them through the ringer. The clothes were then hung on an outside line to dry. The clothes always had the fresh smell of the outdoors. There were paper dress patterns that you purchased along with material, so you could make your own dresses and clothes. *Can-Cans* were also popular at this time. They were skirts that flared out. For originality, the movie *Grease* incorporated these. My sisters used sugar water to make their *Can-Cans* keep their shape. Four-buckle, black boots were common. I remember also that black and white photographs were the most common and inexpensive. You dropped off your roll of photographs, and two weeks later they were ready. Kodak was the household word in photography and eight millimeter movie film was becoming popular.

As would be expected, I have seen the economy change drastically in my life as well. As a child, when you purchased a bicycle that was on display or an item which needed to be put together, you paid the regular price of the item if it was already assembled. But, you received a ten percent discount on an item, such as a bicycle, if it was unassembled and you had to put it together yourself. Nowadays the reverse happens, you pay regular price and they sell it to you unassembled and expect you to assemble it. Also back then, when you purchased something at a store or gas station you received stamps, "Green Stamps" were the most common and were licked and pasted in books. Completed books were then redeemed for various items. Households had to be thrifty in those days because they only had a single income and you needed a good qualification for credit. Therefore, businesses had to entice consumers to purchase with extra incentives. Using stamps based on purchases was a good way to accomplish this.

Service has taken a downward trend since I was a child. When I was young, service was extended to filling your gas tank, washing your windows, and checking your oil, all free. Service station attendants came out to your car and pumped the gasoline for you. The attendant would also check your tire pressure as part of the service just for purchasing gasoline. Today we fill our own vehicles with gas, clean our own windows, and check our own oil and tire pressure, then walk in and pay the attendant or use a credit card at the pump.

When I was young, automobiles did not have cup holders. You could purchase a plastic holder that had an arm to slide between your door and window to keep the holder in place. Automobiles had velvet interiors and large manual steering wheels, because most automobiles did not have power steering. A car radio, power steering, and power brakes were options that cost more. They were not standard. All automobiles during this era had rear wheel drive. There were drive-in movies which, at the time, you only paid per car instead of by occupants in the car. Few drive-in movies remain today.

Automobiles also used different tires (snow tires) in the winter with deep threads to have better traction in snow. There were also summer and winter automobile coolants. Fall was a busy time with storm windows to be put on homes, and winter tires and anti-freeze changed in your automobile. Automobile gasoline cost only 24.9 and 25.9 (cents), or 32.9 a gallon for premium which was referred to as "Ethyl" (short for ethylene which gave it more combustion power). Regular gasoline was the norm. It contained lead compounds which helped reduce the "knocking" in engines of the day. Most automobile windows were cranked up manually. Also at various service stations, if you put in so many gallons you got a free drinking glass. You could very easily build a set of glassware this way.

As previously mentioned, in late fall, outside windows were replaced with storm windows, which had glass instead of screen. Even though these windows were put on outside of the main windows to add insulation, they always had air leaks which would cause ice to build up on the inside window. This build up of ice was called "Jack-Frost" and created interesting designs. During this time also, most homes used kerosene space heaters for heating in the winter. Others burned coal. Those houses had a characteristic metal door at their foundation where coal was delivered. The distinctive rumbling of the coal tumbling down the ramp to the basement could be heard all the way down the block.

In school, when it was too cold for recess or outside activities, we played group games in the gym for physical education. We played a game called *Pum-Pum-Pull-Away*; as we went to pull you away we would chant, *Pum-Pum-Pull-Away, come-or-we-will-pull-you-away!* Another game was called *Bombardment.* We would all line up against a gym wall with two classmates in the middle of the gym with basketballs. When the teacher blew a whistle or shouted, everyone that was lined up against the wall, would run to the other side of the gym. The two classmates in the middle would throw the basketball at people's legs below the knee to put them "out." This would continue until there were no students left to be "put out." I prided myself at his game and at times was one of the last to be put out.

In class I remember the distinct smell of the mimeographed paper used for worksheets and tests. Your natural tendency was to smell it first as it was handed to you. Because of the fluids used to duplicate the sheets it gave the paper a distinct odor until it had all evaporated. This was the pre-copier era.

Stamp and coin collecting were also common past-times for kids and adults during this era. Collecting stamps and coins taught organization, familiarization with other languages, geography, and minting and printing processes, and the proper care of items. In today's society video games have only partially replaced some of these learned skills.

Also, as a child, I remember crying rooms in theatres and churches, where mothers would go with a child, or bored toddler, so they would not disturb the rest of the people. My Saturday morning chore was to burn the weekly garbage, which I did in a rusty old 55 gallon drum, set on several bricks to allow air passage through holes drilled in its bottom.

My grandparents, who lived on a farm, did not have running water or plumbing. Water was obtained from a well just down the hill from their house. They would carry pails of water for drinking, cooking, and bathing. To have a drink of water, you went to the pantry and used a long handled ceramic coated metal dipper to dip into a pail of water covered by a clean dish towel. My grandparents also had an outhouse complete with a Sears catalogue.

I remember when my grandparents got their first telephone, I was five years old. It was an old wooden crank "party-line" wall phone. To use the telephone, you would first lift the receiver then crank a handle to be connected. And long distance calls would go through a local operator. The term "party-line" meant that you would be on a circuit of several other homes in the area. You would listen for your distinct ring to know that it was a call for you. This was a live circuit, if you were having a conversation anyone on the party-line could listen in – and they did. Telephone numbers back then begin with a word or alphabetical prefix. We had the phone number RE8-2765.

Also at this time my grandparents were converted to electricity. Prior to that, when we would visit my grandparents' farm, kerosene lamps were lighted as it became dusk. I remember especially the tall silver mantle lamp that was in the center of a vintage round wooden table. It lit up the whole room. In the small town where I was born and partially raised, Saturday afternoons and evenings were filled with activity and shopping. Farmers would come into town to purchase their supplies for the week or month. My sisters would purchase dress patterns to make their own dresses, and sheet music to learn the latest songs. Few stores were open on Sundays.

I remember purchasing candy cigarettes and small wax imitation Coke bottles with *Kool-Aid* inside. You would bite off the wax cap and drink the *Kool-Aid*. Many times you even chewed the wax. You could buy candy for a penny. Soda pop machines dispensed glass bottles. I also purchased five-cent packs of baseball cards that had a pink rectangle of bubble gum inside. Bread came packaged in waxed paper. Milk was delivered to the home in glass bottles that had cardboard stoppers. The cream would settle on the inside of the stopper and was usually licked off by a young member of the family. We were made to swallow a teaspoon of cod-liver oil to keep us healthy, and when we were sick, we were given orange-flavored chewable baby aspirin. My grandmother would give you a spoonful of brandy if you had a cold.

Most mothers were home-makers and prepared all family meals. The few times we ate at a restaurant was a treat. We could have *malted-milks* and California hamburgers (they had lettuce and tomato). At a soda fountain you could order a nickel Coke, which was given to you in a Coca-Cola glass, and if you wanted, you could have a little cherry put in it to make it a Cherry Coke. Soda pop straws were made of wax-coated paper. It was popular for girls to press these between their fingers while chanting, "He loves me, he loves me not" until you got to the end of the straw. Before you used your straw to drink, it was customary to tear off one end of the thin paper covering of the straw, and with a full breath, propel the thin outer cover like a missile into the air.

The fore-runner of the microwave dinner was the "TV Dinner." A TV dinner consisted of a thin aluminum plate with one large and two smaller depressions. There could be chicken in the large depression, peas or corn in one of the smaller depressions, and usually mashed potatoes or tater-tots in the other depression. The whole tray would be heated in the oven. Once it was baked, you would remove a thin aluminum cover and eat the meal out of its container. TV trays were also invented to accommodate the meal. They were small foldable trays that could be set up for each family member to eat their TV dinner while watching television. Ice cubes were made in aluminum trays with a handle in the center that you pulled to break out the cubes. During this time also, it was not unusual to have an encyclopedia or vacuum salesman come knocking at your door. Also common at the time were visits by "The Fuller Brush" man who also sold wares door-to-door.

As children, we played with *Lincoln* and *American logs*, which were made of cedar and cut so they could be interlocked to make toy log cabins and buildings. We had cork pop guns, *Tinker Toys* and erector sets. Most of our toys were made of metal or wood, and sometimes plastic. We had roller skates that attached to our shoes that were tightened or loosened with a key. And to make our bikes sound like motorcycles, we attached playing cards to our bikes so they would be brushed by the spokes to make noise. Children would play a game where a ball would be rolled over the roof of a shed or small building, with each throw they would yell to friends on the other side, "Oly-oly-oxen-free" then run to the other side. Decisions were made by saying, "Eeny-meeny-miney-mo."

There was also a game called *Jumping Jacks*, played mostly by girls, where the player would throw a dozen metal Jacks on the ground then bounce a small rubber ball, while trying to pick up as many "Jacks" as possible before the ball hit the ground. Children also played marbles, and jump rope. Winters seemed snowy and cold, and summers warm and humid, with few weeks passing without one or more thunderstorms. Whenever there was a change in weather it was blamed on "Sputnik" the satellite the Russians had orbiting the Earth, and on all the missiles they kept shooting up into space.

During these years there were fix-it shops, and television repairmen. Most home appliances were repaired instead of bought and thrown away when they no longer worked. Technology was at a level that would explode in just a few short decades. Cameras used blue flash bulbs that created a bright flash of light for taking pictures. Tape recorders were reel-to-reel, and record players were called "Hi fi's" (High Fidelity) and played "33$^{1/2}$" revolutions per minute (rpm's) or "78s", or smaller records referred to as "45s." A man on television named Art Linkletter used the early form of a computer to match persons for compatibility when I was eight years old. Computers filled a room then, and were rudimentary at best, compared to today's technology. In 1969 I watched the moonlanding on television.

When I was a child, mothers would expose their children to neighborhood children who had what was considered common childhood diseases (Measles, Mumps, Whooping Cough, and Chicken Pox). These diseases were considered part of childhood. Moms would hasten the process by exposing their children to other children who had the diseases. I remember in third grade I contracted all of these diseases and missed a lot of school. We have since eradicated most of them. When we had a fever, our temperature was taken with a glass and mercury thermometer which took a full minute of being kept under your tongue, to obtain a reading. Also in those days, doctors came to your home. I was very surprised after we had moved to the city, to learn that doctors did not come to your home, instead, you had to go to their office or clinic.

As a child I sometimes took the mercury from electric motion switches to play with, rolling it around in my hand. If that same event were to occur today in a school, a special squad in protective gowns would be called, the school evacuated and a bill for thousands of dollars mailed to the school for services. At age sixteen, in 1966, I walked into Sears Department Store, the sports department, and paid $29.95 for an 8mm Mauser Rifle with 50 rounds of ex-military, steel-jacketed ammunition. Other than the sales slip there was no other paperwork required, nor a parent signature needed. I had the cash to pay for my purchase, and that is all that was needed. I did not even have to pay a state sales tax on my purchase, as we do today since sales taxes were not yet enacted. Ironically, this was only three years after President John F. Kennedy had been assassinated with a similar high-power rifle.

When I was a child, by law, attorneys could not publicly advertise their services. Banks would close everyday at three in the afternoon, so they could do their bookwork, since everything was done manually on ledger sheets. People dressed with thin ties and wore hats as part of their dress. Everyone dressed more formally. If going to a movie or event they would come dressed in suits and ties, and in evening dresses, not casual attire. I also remember that until the early 1960s there used to be two separate want-ad sections for jobs in newspapers. One section was jobs for women, and the other, jobs for men. The roles of women began to change at about this time as they began to have dual careers.

By the 1970s, traditional terminology began to change. The Personnel Department became Human Resources; Secretary became Administrative Assistant; Mongolism was referred to as Down's Syndrome; General Practitioner became Family Practice; Gay replaced Queer or Homosexual; and classical musicians had the distinction of being called "Long Hairs", until the band, *The Beatles* changed that.

Until I was eleven years old, I did not know the daily convenience of an invention by Mr. Crapper – the flush toilet. Oh yes, I knew they existed, but I did not have the convenience of their use in our own home. We lived at the edge of a small town in a large old house originally built in 1890. A kerosene space heater sat near one wall of our living room. We did not have hot water, only cold water which froze several times during a typical winter. My mother would walk the length of the pipe in the basement heating it with a candle.

For convenience, a porcelain covered metal pot was kept in the house, usually under a bed or in a closet. It was the dubious task of the sustaining family member to carry out the pot each day to be emptied in the "outhouse" outdoors. My sisters had the task of emptying the pot before me. Then my oldest sister graduated and went to hair-stylist school, which was called "Beauty School" at that time. A year later, my other sister went to the city to work and attend college. This left "me" to empty the pot. It was a passed down tradition from the oldest sibling to the younger.

I could not approach this anomaly as I did the dish drying experiment, when my mother decided to have me help wipe the dishes at the finish of each supper. I purposely let a few pieces slip out of my hand and the "honor" was taken away from me. But this tactic could not carry over to the pot situation. I remember it well; oh, the pouring of that effluent into those old circular sawed holes of the outhouse!

I remember one evening, my sister in her sleep, sat on a roll of toilet paper placed next to the pot instead of the pot itself. By morning the toilet paper roll had swelled to twice its size. It was the laugh of the family for quite some years later. Since there was no indoor plumbing, a "slop pail" was kept beneath the kitchen sink. This too had to be emptied several times a day, but that is another story.

What people refer to when they say, "The good old days" is that those days were simpler, less complex, and people relied on each other more. There were fewer laws and legislation to complicate society.

PIONEER INGENUITY

At the beginning of the last century (1900s) when groups of immigrants settled in the United States there was little social help for them. Cities were crowded with immigrants. They survived by their ingenuity and reliance on each other. These early groups relied on one another for help and would barter their services. A carpenter would lend his services in exchange for the expertise of a mechanic, or just for food. Therefore, money being in short supply, did not have to change hands.

One method some early groups used was to have a lottery. Families would periodically have a lottery where each family paid a small amount for the opportunity to win. They would draw a name and one of the families would win the lottery. In this way early families could pay for a needed item or repair, or improvement that cost more than they could afford normally. Bank loans were difficult to obtain without collateral. With a lottery everyone had the same chance to win just by purchasing an inexpensive ticket.

Another way some early groups were able to have the luxury of an automobile was through community ownership and sharing. Several families who could not afford an automobile could independently pool their resources to purchase one. They took turns, usually by weekly allotments to use the automobile. One week, one family would have the use of the automobile, the next week a different family, and so forth in an unending schedule. Maintenance of the vehicle was also shared.

Cooperatives were another way early Americans benefited from group pooling of resources. Many co-ops to this day exist especially in rural areas. Farmer's co-ops, rural electric co-ops, and credit unions, are a few examples. Pioneers had a great pride in themselves and their abilities. We Americans need to keep the spirit and ingenuity of our pioneers alive.

CHAPTER TWELVE
TO OUR YOUTH AND OUR FUTURE

The significant problems we face today cannot be solved at the same level of thinking we were at when we created them.
~ Albert Einstein

In most modern politics, unfortunately, it may truly be said that those who make history never know history. ~ G. K. Chesterton

This book is but one of many on the subject of Personality Styles, but only one of a few that have tried to explain the basis of politics and cognitive political ideology through Personality Styles. Ultimately, Personality Style traits will be better understood and defined by the base of life, the DNA molecule. Genetic engineering will play a significant role in the future micro-analysis of this study.

In this writing many things have been discussed. Many things to think about, ponder, and take action on. Some things are frightening and make you fearful for the future. But, hopefully this book will leave you with the reality that mankind, since his inception, has continued to persist through epidemics, wars, famine, natural disasters, and chaos, and will continue to persist. With ongoing technology and persistence, mankind will overcome anything put in his way. But all generations need to be aware, informed, and take individual initiative to maintain the freedoms we have in America that we take for granted.

If this book has made others aware enough to take action, then this has all been worthwhile, and not just lost in the annals of the 160,000 books published each year in America. If the readers of this book take a few minutes to reflect on what they have read, and vow to make change, the research and compiling of this book will have been well worth it. The easiest way to make change is to VOTE.

There are many things in the book I have promoted for change. The power to make these changes will have to come from individual citizen effort, at the grass roots level of involvement, formed collectively into a movement, and from the sovereignty of states to make major constitutional changes.

Americans should be ready to change the following:

- **PERSONALITY STYLES.** We need to be aware of Personality Styles to better understand our fellow human beings, socially as well as politically.

- **EDUCATION.** American citizens need to be educated and motivated at the grass roots level to take responsibility to guide this country, and its elected representatives, in a positive direction. If each American would devote half an hour a day to current issues and events and discuss them with their family, America would be a safer and freer nation, with more educated voters electing better persons to represent them.

  Many Americans need to also re-evaluate their political ideologies. They need to verify to themselves that what they believe in is still viable. Things change, and parties change. Long term members of parties and political associations need to reinforce their reason why they are a member. They need to look deeper than just the surface, into such entities, when making this decision. I find that many people do not have a solid idea why they vote the way they do or what motivates them to select one candidate over the other.

- **THIRD PARTY.** America desperately needs an established third party – a recognized national middle party in America. Not just a one issue or interest party, but a party that can effectively represent that vast majority of persons in the center. As citizens we need more than two predominant choices in our representation. Just as balance exists in nature, human beings need social and political balance.

- **TERM LIMITS, INTEREST GROUPS, LOBBYISTS, EARMARKS, SMALLER GOVERNMENT.** We need to establish term limits for all elected politicians. Longevity in office breeds corruption. The approval of Congress by the general public, whom Congress should be serving, is extremely low. The abuses heard on the daily news, about senators and representatives who have been consistently elected for decades, are unbelievable. The power they amass with their long tenure is easily misused. The longer in office, the more out of touch they become with their constituents, and are more prone to their own personal agendas. Presidential second terms are generally less effective and productive. Term limits have worked in other nations. Honduras has written in their constitution that a president can only serve one term of four years. This constitutional dictate has been challenged but remains steadfast. It is crucial that this also becomes an amendment to our own US Constitution. No elected president or legislator should have more than one term.

We need to also eliminate the slanted legislation of our representatives by ridding them of interest groups and lobbyists. We need to eliminate all outside influences on our representatives. It is crucial that we take this flaw away from those making decisions for us. Interest groups and the media are electing our presidents. Direct voting is possible with todays technology. We need to have as many issues directly decided upon by each voter. In this way everyone can directly affect a bill or issue, not have the decision waiver on an intermediary; i.e. an elected legislator.

We need to seriously consider a one-house, unicameral government. We must reduce the size of government. Unicameral government has been successful in the state of Nebraska since 1937. When it was instituted, "Legislative membership went from 133 in the bicameral to 43 in the new single house – nearly a 70 percent reduction. Also, the one-house system was more efficient than its predecessor. The last bicameral session in 1935 ran 110 days, passed 192 bills and cost $202,593. The first unicameral session two years later ran 98 days, passed 214 bills and cost $103,445. Another unique aspect of Nebraska's legislature is its nonpartisanship"[1]

With the events occurring at the writing of this book, our nation is prime for change. There are ever growing Libertarian, centrist, and grass roots Tea Party movements, and grave concerns in the minds of citizens for our failing economy and national safety.

Our federal government and presidency has gotten too powerful, much of this power needs to be given back to the citizens. There needs to be more citizen groups making decisions on issues that affect all Americans. The presidency has been gaining more and more power over the last 100 years, and especially during the administration of FDR. We need more citizen groups making decisions. Take government out of party control and return many of its processes to the people. I could never understand why presidents get to appoint their own attorney generals. If this were not the case, the controversy over President Obama's true birth certificate would have been solved once and for all by the attorney general, the person that should be looking into such matters.

We need more citizen groups involved in the political decision-making process so such things as selection of an attorney general, supreme court judges, and the census, to name a few, are taken out of partisan control. Some believe repeal of the 17th Amendment would help balance irresponsible spending by reversing the selection process for Senators, and tie their budgets back to the states, as was the original case. We need to keep major decisions out of the hands of power hungry presidents, senators, and representatives.

Our Constitution is a living constitution; therefore, it allows for change. On most of these changes the citizenry and states will have to step forth, Congress will not consider voting for any of these major issues because it will jeopardize their power.

- **PREFERENTIAL BENEFITS SHOULD BE ELIMINATED.**
Put senators, representatives, the president and all other persons in elected positions in line with the rest of the populous with regard to a retirement plan and healthcare. Why should we pay for their benefits when we also have to pay for our own? School districts and corporations are instituting this balance, with health insurance policies being equal, and the same from the top down. Why can't our elected officials do the same?

Upon retirement, the average citizen that has paid into Social Security all his life will receive about $1,000 a month. What is disconcerting is that members of Congress will receive several times this amount. If members of Congress had to rely only on Social Security, they would fix this disparity fast. Congress should pay for its own health insurance like the rest of us have to. This is another taxpayer benefit to them. It was not surprising that not one Congress person wanted to be part of the Nationalized Health Care plan that President Obama initiated. Congressman John Fleming (R-LA) even proposed an amendment that would require those in both houses of Congress to be part of the same healthcare they forced upon us. Congressman Fleming is a physician.

Neither should Congress be able to vote for their raises. We cannot, why should they? Congress has had a history of receiving automatic raises every January 1st. This was the case in 2008 when they received a 2.5 percent increase. Then again in 2009, in an economy where people were losing jobs and exhausting their savings, Congress received a 2.8 percent increase. All laws should apply to all citizens, equally, from the president on down.

Senators, representatives, and elected officials are employed by the people through elections and are put in office to represent us fairly, and be respectful of our tax burdens and safety. Why shouldn't we be in charge of their performance review? They may even listen to us then! We also need to protect Social Security as any other retirement plan is protected under established laws, and remove it as a federal revenue asset. It should not be considered part of the revenue budget, but protected from sticky legislative hands.

- **LEGITIMATE NEWS REPORTING.** There needs to be better ethics followed in news reporting. The media should not continue to hide behind the First Amendment. We need to bring reporters, journalists, and media companies to legal challenges if they report slanted, bias information, which destroys a family or individual, or puts our safety at risk. To most, this is criminal negligence.

The media must move away from sensationalism and move to investigative journalism.

- **ELECTIONS.** We need to evaluate if the Electoral College is still viable. It was needed in a time when the American population was less educated and communication was rudimentary. Now, with the outcomes of campaigns instantaneous, we no longer need to employ an Electoral College. We should not report state by state wins until the very end of the campaign in national elections, after all the western states have cast and counted their ballots. We must eliminate any potential of voter disparity and fraud.

A president elected by the people should be a representative equally to all citizens. An elected president should not represent their party by supporting same party candidates. A president should represent all the people, and not use their position to unfairly promote their party. True bipartisanship is a sign of a good president.

- **THREATS TO AMERICA AND OUR WAY OF LIFE.** As a nation, we must also acknowledge that we have enemies. In a liberal society, it is all about peace, happiness, and socialist equality, just as we see in the psyche of the Promoter personality. But we are in different times, with enemies among us. We cannot continue to believe that our existence is safe, happy, and liberal. Every American should be aware of our enemies both internally and abroad. The media also needs to downgrade its liberal stance, and be more realistic and proactive concerning the intentions of other nations, dictatorships, cultures, and terrorist groups in our world community. It is unfortunate that a liberal society leaves you vulnerable with reduced military. This opens our nation to terrorism, and being unprepared for disasters (like hurricane Katrina). I dread the day when a terrorist organization is able to assemble a "suitcase nuke," and destroys a good portion of New York City or Washington D.C.

All Americans need to understand the serious threat of terrorism. The hatred fundamentalists have for America should send a warning to every American citizen. Terrorists are already among us, always in waiting for an opportunity to harm us. There has been a declared war by Islamic fundamentalists against all non-Islamic peoples and nations since 1979. The goal of the fundamentalist movement is to convert, or to kill, every non-Islamic person on Earth. They will simply not just go away, but will continue to persist in their goal (See, "Terrorism" in the Appendix).

To maintain our nation's internal strength and oneness we need to maintain only one language, English. It has always been the national language spoken in The United States of America. My immigrant grandparents understood and followed this. My grandmother taught herself English after she had come to America. We should not fragment, or undermine, our nation by instituting a second national language. Any nation that has done this has suffered complications and internal strife. We need to be steadfast and not allow a secondary language to complicate the infrastructure of our nation. Whether a citizen, visitor, or an emigrant, all persons in this nation need to utilize our national written and spoken language, English.

- **IMMIGRATION.** We have always been a tolerant society. We accept peoples from all nations because of political and religious wars, famines, and wars in other nations that the United States has been involved in. Most of our population can trace its roots as immigrants. We have allowed immigration since the inception of our nation. Immigration can generally have a positive impact on a nation, but can also cause concerns. In a balanced society, the young, pre-career teenagers take the jobs at the minimum wage level. They work the jobs that more tenured persons do not wish to do. A growing number of retired and elderly persons are also doing these types of jobs to earn extra income. Immigration influx can upset this delicate balance. Also, with natural resources dwindling because of normal population growth, our natural resources and tillable lands are being affected. At this writing, the population of the United States is over 300 million persons.

  America is still the number one sought-after country for immigration because of its freedom, economy, and opportunity. We need to make known our needs, not just accept anyone into our nation as a potential liability. Just as other nations have learned, such as Canada, which makes it known what type of emigrant they wish: engineers, scientists, chemists, etc. We already have over 300 million people in America utilizing our dwindling resources. We must be more selective and advertise "our needs" to potential emigrants. As populations the world over continue to grow simultaneously with reduced resources, we need to be selective in our needs. This will also keep us competitive as a global member (See, "Illegal Immigration" in the Appendix).

- **FOREIGN AID.** We should always be a willing nation and people when it comes to helping other people in need. When international disasters occur, we need to help. But at the same time, we need to re-evaluate the plethora of foreign aid that we give each year to other nations. Many, who even condemn us as they take our aid, predominantly because of the conditions attached to the aid. In the last several decades many nations have reached a higher standard, in part due to better education, technology and communication (the internet especially), and global commerce. Our aid dollars could easily be used domestically, or by reducing and restricting payments to these foreign entities, could help our budget deficit.

Throughout history there has always been one group more civilized, more commerce savvy, and more advanced than others and therefore, able to pillage and plunder the others. This has been true of all the great civilizations. But they have usually fallen because of internal strife and upheaval. What is happening today with a world dictated by technology, communication, scientific advances, and one global economy is that all other peoples, cultures, and political states are developing and growing to the same level as the United States. Therefore, we as a nation must rely on competition through good education, technology, and innovativeness to stay ahead. Nations can no longer plunder, and there are no new lands to explore and develop.

In the first decade of the new millennium America is in a "social civil war." It has crested with over four decades of moving ever to the left. The liberal left, with many decades of socializing America, is now looking to globalism and world government. This social civil war is between those who want to continue promoting a liberal-socialist agenda to ultimately absorb the United States, and then the world, with a globalist government ("One World Order"), against those who wish to keep the freedoms that Americans have enjoyed for over 200 years. This is taking place as you read this print.

At the surface it is a quiet revolution. It may be subtle, but it is ever advancing. Things at the surface may still seem routine and normal. You see your neighbors going to work, mowing their yards, shopping for groceries, and their kids going to school. But, ideology is constantly at the fringe and is an ever creeping menace. Ideologically and socially we are at war. Our freedom is at stake. Just like the populous was unaware of the beginnings of the Nazi movement in Germany in the early 1930s because of the seemingly benign routine.

This is not being likened to Nazism, but the same mood and complacency of the voters is similar. We have to get the word out to our fellow Americans and educate the populous that have been indoctrinated into liberal-socialist dogma for decades. American citizens must understand the restrictive course we are on. They must understand the only society that will survive is a fiscally responsible society based on individual effort. Freedom does not come free, it has a cost. Maria A. "Hansi" Hirschmann, who escaped from Nazi Germany states, "Freedom works through individuals, not the masses."

Hopefully, some answers and direction to these concerns have been presented in this book. The most important message I hope to have provided is that everyone has a voice and should speak out. We are in a liberal abyss. We must first work our way out of this abyss before anything else can function. This liberal oversensitization has breached institutions, the family, and the ultimate future security of the United States. Look at how education curriculum and emphasis has changed in the last four decades. True freedom should bring prosperity, not socialism.

Conservatives have been demonized by the political left, our youth indoctrinated to liberal ideology; and in the left's anti-American criticism, has proclaimed patriotism as bigotry and racism. The same system of checks and balances put in place by our founding fathers to protect us from unconstitutional mandates being passed (Healthcare, Cap and Trade, etc.) is the same system that allows arrogance, greed, and the unquenchable lust for power to develop in our elected representatives. They have undermined these checks and balances to create the problems and concerns we see today.

Our only recourse is smaller government, less power to the presidency and Congress, and more decision making coming directly from the citizenry. The Romans had a strong Tribune in their system to limit this abuse of power. The Tribune worked for the common citizen, they protected the citizen's lives and property, and had the power to overturn elections, laws, and Roman senate decrees. Ironically, Tribunes served only one year and were required to always keep their home available for visitors, even during the night, and were not allowed to be more than one day's journey from Rome. We as citizens must always be aware that any system can be corrupted; therefore, we must be more responsible and informed. We must be the real checks-and-balances with our government and our system. Our founding fathers based their new government on an understanding of human nature and world history.

How will the next generations deal with liberal bias and socialism? Will they overcome its grasping tentacles and seek truth and reality? With this book I will not change the hard liberal or the hard right conservative's mind, but I hope to influence those in-between these two extremes. Hopefully, by making the populous more aware and prompting it to action, this endeavor will have been worthwhile. The only way for the people to take back their government is through educating themselves and through grass roots ideology and involvement. A nation, or any political entity, is never very far away from anarchy – just let a few of the wrong people in office and it will happen. Ronald Reagan stated:

"We are always only one generation away from losing what we have."

The liberal political spectrum is relying upon citizens not to step out of their social indenturement the left has put them in. Those on the left are very vocal and, "like to give it out, but do not like to receive it." They think themselves never wrong, are self-focused, and obsessed with sensitivity to the point of detriment. We must move our youth away from the mentality of social gifting and entitlements, and move them instead into being more independent and believing in themselves.

Maintaining freedom is not easy. It requires sacrifices. The United States has been challenged many times over the course of its existence, and its citizens have always stepped up to the challenge and protected it. Now the threat is from within. Our nation is under attack on several fronts both internally and externally; socialism from within, and fundamentalist terrorists from cells within our nation, ready to attack, and terrorists groups and despots from without. The United States has always had petty despots keep trying to prod us with thorns, but now they are able to use nuclear weapons. The world is more than ever in an integrated global community, where one neighbor's political and economic problems can affect other members in this global existence.

In the words of John F. Kennedy, "A revolution is coming – a revolution which will be peaceful if we are wise enough; compassionate if we care enough; successful if we are fortunate enough – but a revolution which is coming whether we will it or not. We can affect its character; we cannot alter its inevitability."

The future belongs to our youth; it is only a matter of how they will change or accept it. Gandhi summarized it best, "We must be the change we wish to see in the world." And as the comedian, George Burns, so aptly put it, "I look to the future because that's where I'm going to spend the rest of my life."

Norman M. Thomas (1884-1968), six-time American Socialist Party candidate, said the following in 1944:

"The American people will never knowingly adopt socialism. But, under the name of *liberalism* they will adopt every fragment of the socialist program, until one day America will be a socialist nation, without knowing how it happened... I no longer need to run as Presidential Candidate for the Socialist Party. The Democrat Party has adopted our platform."

168

APPENDIX

CONTACTING YOUR REPRESENTATIVE

The following is how to correspond to United States Senators and Representatives. When contacting a senator or representative always list your return mailing address.

TO A SENATOR BY MAIL or E-MAIL

The Honorable <Name>
United States Senate
Washington, D.C. 20510

Dear Senator < NAME>

TO A SENATE COMMITTEE CHAIR

<Name of Committee>
The Honorable <Name>
United States Senate
Washington, D.C. 20510

TO A REPRESENTATIVE BY MAIL or E-MAIL

The Honorable <Name>
United States House of Representatives
Washington, D.C. 20510

Dear Representative <Name>

BY PHONE
(202) 224 – 3121

QUICK METHOD TO DETERMINE YOUR PERSONALITY & ASSOCIATE STYLES

Check only <u>one item</u> in each row across, then total at the bottom. Go with your first thought, move quickly through and do not concentrate on any one item.

1) ____Florals	____Geometrics	____Solids	____Plaids
2) ____Open Gestures	____Set Apart	____Quiet	____Shy
3) ____Outgoing	____Competitive	____Perfectionist	____Content
4) ____Sociable	____Independent	____Analytic	____Friendly
5) ____Pastel Colors	____Bold Colors	____Basic Colors	____Earth Tones
6) ____Positive	____Aggressive	____Organized	____Adaptable
7) ____Soft Hearted	____Direct	____Considerate	____Listener
8) ____Dressing Up	____Making a Statement	____Fitting In	____Comfortable
9) ____Optimistic	____Confident	____Dedicated	____Balanced
10)____Delicate Jewelry	____Bold Jewelry	____Basic Jewelry	____No Jewelry
11)____Changeable	____Sure	____Predictable	____Dependable
12)____Love to Shop	____Love to Find Unique Items	____Make an Investment	____Hate to Shop

A. _____ Totals B. _____ Totals C. _____ Totals D. _____ Totals

My predominant Personality Style _____.

My Associate Personality Style _____.

Original source of above table unknown

Item 1b

QUICK METHOD TO DETERMINE YOUR PERSONALITY & ASSOCIATE STYLES

Check only <u>one item</u> in each row across, then total at the bottom. Go with your first thought, move quickly through and do not concentrate on any one item.

EXAMPLE & KEY

1) ____Florals	____Geometrics	**X** Solids	____Plaids
2) ____Open Gestures	**X** Set Apart	____Quiet	____Shy
3) ____Outgoing	**X** Competitive	____Perfectionist	____Content
4) **X** Sociable	____Independent	____Analytic	____Friendly
5) ____Pastel Colors	____Bold Colors	**X** Basic Colors	____Earth Tones
6) ____Positive	**X** Aggressive	____Organized	____Adaptable
7) **X** Soft Hearted	____Direct	____Considerate	____Listener
8) ____Dressing Up	____Making a Statement	**X** Fitting In	____Comfortable
9) ____Optimistic	**X** Confident	____Dedicated	____Balanced
10) ____Delicate Jewelry	____Bold Jewelry	**X** Basic Jewelry	____No Jewelry
11) ____Changeable	**X** Sure	____Predictable	____Dependable
12) ____Love to Shop	**X** Love to Find Unique Items	____Make an Investment	____Hate to Shop

A. __2__ Totals B. __6__ Totals C. __4__ Totals D. __0__ Totals

(PROMOTER)   (DIRECTOR)   (ANALYZER)   (SUPPORTER)

My predominant Personality Style ____*DIRECTOR*____ .

My Associate Personality Style ____*ANALYZER*____ .

Original source of above table unknown

Item 2 Illegal Immigration
There is no doubt that illegal immigration has its price, and detriment to a nation. It affects our existence in many ways. Our ever growing liberal immigration policies are counterproductive to the sovereignty and safety of America. Tax consequences of illegal immigration include: annual welfare and social assistance (food stamps, free school lunches, Medicaid), and primary and secondary education. Ancillary to this are the lost wages for American citizens, especially our youth just starting out, because of jobs taken by illegal immigrants. Then, there is the cost of maintaining incarcerated illegal immigrants. Illegal immigrants also send money home, which undermines our economy. Other concerns are that illegal drugs and terrorists are also crossing our borders.

As you can see, the simple act of walking over our border has severe tax and safety consequences to each American. Illegal immigration costs the American taxpayer not only security issues, but billions of dollars a year in taxes. As an aside to the above, in 2008 the US Senate voted to extend Social Security Benefits to illegal aliens. During the Housing Crises that same year, it was reported by Housing and Urban Development (HUD) that five million illegal aliens bought houses with fake social security numbers.

Ironically, Presidents Hoover, Truman & Eisenhower all ordered the deportation of illegal aliens in order to create more jobs for Americans. President Hoover did this during the Great Depression, and President Truman deported over two million after World War Two to create jobs for returning servicemen. In 1954 President Eisenhower also had illegal aliens deported to help the economy and US Citizens in the workforce.

An article in a national magazine during the writing of this book made it obvious the degree to which towns in Northern Mexico rely on illegal immigration as part of their economy. Mexican towns along the United States border have to invite participants from other towns to have such annual events as the rodeo, because most of the young males have left for illegal immigration into the United States. When boys turn fifteen, they go across the border. Because it is becoming riskier and more costly, once in the United States they rarely return to their hometowns. The lack of males is changing their social structure.

Item 3 Terrorism
Terrorism and Islamic fundamentalism are a reality in today's world. In 1979 Islamic religious leaders declared a religious war against

the non-Islamic world. The greatest atrocity done by a foreign organization by Islamic fundamentalists on U.S. soil is what is now referred to as 911. How do we deal with such extremists who only want to see us dead?

The old saying goes, "People who want to share their religious views with you, seldom want you to share yours with them." Things will not change ideologically with Islamic fundamentalists until their culture changes. They are born into hate, grow up in hate, are taught hate in school and are rewarded by their culture when they commit an atrocity to infidels in the name of Allah. They think the way they are told to, because they have been indoctrinated to do so since childhood. Things have to change, and drastically. The only way I see this happening is if they have a modern prophet to let them know the error of their ways. Their views of other non-Islamic cultures have to be changed, and their religion needs to have a prophetic scrutiny.

Things may change, but slowly, and at the cost of many deaths, as more Muslims speak out against their own fundamentalists. This has been the case with Nonie Darwish and Brigitte Gabriel. Both were raised in Islamic culture, but saw the differences and renounced their native culture. In their head-on approach they have helped to awaken America to its fate, and in so doing, have also made other individuals of Islamic culture take a harder look at themselves. Western culture, with its tolerance of all religions and peoples, is a good experience for followers of Islam, who in their own culture have not known any other way but hate of the non-Islamic world.

If you watch a bully in the school yard, nothing changes until someone stands up to him. This is what we need to do until terrorists and fundamentalists are able to take a good look at themselves and attempt to change their ways, and their indifferent destruction and slaughter of those who do not believe as they do. Otherwise, they will appear as a devil incarnate to the rest of the non-Islamic world. Passive liberals, and do-gooders, by their very nature in the name of sensitivity and empathy, will allow terrorism to overtake our nation and culture.

Islamic fundamentalism is a religious war, to make the entire world Islamic with no tolerance for other religions or peoples. Islamic extremists consider non-Islamic peoples to be infidels. They do not wish to understand our culture, our religion, our traditions, or freedoms. They only wish to know how to overcome us and change the entire world to Islam and Sharia law for their own selfish reasons.

The liberalism that we are going through is an advantage for terrorists and extremists because we are a less questioning society and are too tolerant. In their strict teachings, followers of Islam abhor many things about American culture, such as the rights given to same sex partners, and our treatment and overall openness to sexual and moral issues. These are all too culturally overwhelming for followers of Islam and its strict teachings. They judge us on our values and culture through these issues.

There have been many attempts and attacks on Americans by Islamic Fundamentalists since 1979, when under the Jimmy Carter administration hostages were held in the American Embassy in Iran. Each administration since has experienced its share of terrorist attacks. Most of these attacks against Americans occurred in other parts of the world, but beginning in the 1990s they occurred within America. New York, especially, with its large population of Semitics, has been a target for terrorists because of the historic hatred of the Jews by Islamic Fundamentalists.

In 1983, during the administration of President Ronald Reagan there was an attack on the American embassy, and the Marine barracks in Beirut, Lebanon. Then in 1988, the in-air Pan-Am flight after takeoff from Lockerbie, Scotland. During President Bill Clinton's administration in 1993, the World Trade Center in New York was carbombed. In 1996, the Khobar Towers military complex was attacked in Dhahran, Saudi Arabia. In 1998 the U.S. embassies in Nairobi, Kenya, and Dares Salaam, Tanzania, were attacked. October 12, 2000 the ship, U.S.S. Cole was bombed in Aden, Yemen. In addition to American lives, many local citizens were also killed in these attacks. During the administration of George W. Bush, the attack of 9-11 occurred in 2001, with hijacked commercial plane attacks on the World Trade Center towers, the Pentagon, and a failed crash in Pennsylvania, originally destined for the White House. Three thousand lives were lost in these attacks.

During President Barack Obama's administration, even though he tried a more passive approach to terrorism, several attempts and attacks occurred in 2009, his first year as President. In Little Rock, Arkansas, a soldier was killed and one wounded by a convert to Islam at a recruiting office. In Fort Hood, Texas, a U.S. Army Major, Nidal Malik Hasan, killed thirteen and wounded thirty. In addition to the failed Christmas bombing of Northwest flight 253, among other significant terrorist attempts in 2009 would be the plot to blow up a train in Penn Station, on Long

Island, and another in New York, to bomb two synagogues and shoot down military cargo planes. There was also a plot to car bomb a Dallas skyscraper, and yet another to blow up a federal building in Springfield, Illinois. The recruiting of new terrorists appears unending.

Terrorists of any movement or nation need to be overcome for the safety and well being of the global environment we all share. The ambiguities of their politics and culture keep terrorists from fully enjoying a state of peace while in this world. It is not normal for a religion or culture to preach, or condone death and the destruction of others. The doctrine of religion should be peace, love, compassion and tolerance. Although there are passages in the Koran that address this, the overriding factor in Islam (especially since 1979) seems to be Jihad (holy war to make Islam the only world religion through whatever means).

There are many books about Islamic Fundamentalism, they are enlightening and are "must reads" for every citizen of this great nation. Two books I would suggest: *NOW THEY CALL ME INFIDEL, Why I Renounced Jihad for America, Israel, and the War on Terror, by Nonie Darwish*, and, *BECAUSE THEY HATE, A Survivor of Islamic Terror Warns America, by Brigitte Gabriel.*

James Madison wrote, "No nation can preserve [or guarantee] its freedom in the midst of continued warfare."

Nuclear Weapons Materials For Terrorists
On April 24, 2008 a significant event took place that the media gave only passing seconds to. It was the Israeli bombing of a nuclear facility under construction in Syria. It was a suspected cooperative effort between Iran and North Korea. This facility was being built to produce fissionable material for making atomic bombs. This would have given the whole Muslim world, especially Islamic terrorists, access to nuclear weapons for their quest to make the world subservient to Islam. This event was not reported with any hype, just quietly unfolded as a routine news clip. But its significance was unfathomable and should have filled a lengthy media investigative report. Their relative disinterest for something that could vaporize tens-of-thousands of people shocked me. At the writing of this book, Iran is processing weapons grade fissionable material.

The nations that have nuclear capability are part of what is referred to as the "Nuclear Club." As of this writing nine nations have successfully detonated nuclear weapons. Five are termed Nuclear Weapons States by the Nuclear Non-Proliferation Treaty (NPT), initiated in 1970. They are the United States, Russia, Great Britain, France, and China. Other nations that have completed nuclear tests are India, Pakistan, and North Korea. North Korea withdrew from NPT in 2003. Israel is also thought to have nuclear weapons capability, and South Africa developed nuclear weapons but disassembled its arsenal before joining NPT.

A Nuclear Weapons Free Zone (NWFZ) was established by the United Nations as an agreement generated by an internationally recognized treaty, to chart the use and development, or deployment of nuclear weapons in a given area. The agreement includes a method of verification and control to enforce individual obligations. The following nations at the time of this writing, are known to have nuclear weapons (listed with first year tested): The United States (1945); Russia (1949); United Kingdom (1952); France (1960); China (1964); India (1974); Pakistan (1998); North Korea (2006); and Israel (c.1979; an undeclared nuclear weapons state). Fortunately, to date, the United States is the only country that has used a nuclear weapon (against Japan during World War Two).

The Scary Effects of Radiation
"The human body is made up of many organs, and each organ of the body is made up of specialized cells. Ionizing radiation can potentially affect the normal operation of these cells."[1] Biological effects of radiation depend on the length of exposure and its intensity. When human tissue is exposed to radiation, its energy removes electrons from atoms and molecules that make up tissue. When radiation strikes a cell of human tissue, it may or may not strike a critical component in the cell, such as the chromosomes. The body is also constantly repairing itself. Therefore, the amount of exposure and the intensity of the radiation are crucial factors. Rapidly dividing, and non-specialized cells are more sensitive to radiation, especially those cells which produce blood.

The first use of an atomic bomb was on Hiroshima, Japan during World War Two. It was dropped August 6, 1945, and detonated 1,900 feet above the city. In that instant an estimated 70,000 people were killed from the blast, heat, and initial radiation, with a like amount of people injured. Others were killed or injured by fires; "The numerous small fires that erupted simultaneously all around the city soon merged into one large firestorm, creating extremely strong winds that blew towards the center of the fire."..."By the end of 1945, because of the lingering effects of radioactive fallout and other after effects, the Hiroshima death toll was probably over 100,000. The five-year death total may have reached or even exceeded 200,000, as cancer and other long-term effects took hold."[2] Never before had such devastation occurred from a single device of war. Since 1945 there have been many advances to more powerful and smaller "weapons of mass destruction." Now we have terrorists threatening to utilize such weapons on cities and populations in America and elsewhere.

When the Hiroshima bomb detonated, all matter was totally vaporized within half a mile. Severe damage occurred up to two miles, and fires were created up to three miles from the blast. In addition to a devastating shock wave, and gamma radiation from the blast, radioactive fallout was also produced. Fallout, consisting of new radioactive elements created by the splitting of the Uranium or Plutonium atoms, combines with dust particles and is carried aloft. Residual radiation, causing *Acute Radiation Syndrome Sickness*, remains in the air, soil, and water for hundreds of hours after the blast. The closer to the center of the blast, the more radiation exposure is received. Entering within one kilometer of the Hiroshima blast site, even 100 hours after the blast, critical doses of residual radiation would have been received. Months after the Hiroshima bomb people died from continued exposure to residual radiation.

A few hours after the explosion, vomiting was the first sign of acute radiation syndrome. Later, a person's hair would either fall out or become very thin and brittle and eventually break off. Vomiting, diarrhea, reduced red blood cells, bleeding, continued hair loss, temporary sterility in males, and opaque eye lenses were the most common symptoms resulting from acute radiation syndrome. If exposure to the radiation was small, not all the symptoms would occur, but with higher doses of radiation, death could occur two or more months after exposure from bone marrow complications. With doses higher yet, death could occur within 10 to 20 days caused by intestinal disorders.

Cancer and genetic abnormalities are potential long term conditions from radiation exposure, and can appear in future generations. A fetus is especially sensitive to radiation since it has rapidly dividing cells (and is most crucial if exposure occurs within the first twenty weeks of pregnancy). Exposure of a fetus to radiation can cause growth retardation, small head and brain size, mental retardation, and childhood cancer.[1, 3] Overall, limiting the dose of radiation minimizes your risk. Radiation exposure, no matter how little, always caries some risk.

Another way a nuclear weapon can cause widespread damage, is if it were used as an Electromagnetic Pulse (EMP) weapon. EMP is caused by a nuclear detonation at high altitude which creates high levels of gamma rays, and free electrons which immediately gravitate to the Earth's magnetic field causing a powerful oscillating current. This electromagnetic pulse could affect an entire continent. The surge would potentially overcharge power lines, telephone wires, electrical components, antennas, communication systems, aircraft and satellites, and anything affected by a strong magnetic field.

Item 4 How To Deal With A Liberal Opponent
- Acknowledge that they will not change.
- Use verifiable data and statistics to blow away their smoke screen.
- Expose their sensitivity bias and defenses; be aware that they will always use these as a hedge against you and other opponents.
- Do not trust them; they will use any means within their grasp to be right or to win.
- They are very vocal, wear them down verbally, get in-their-face, go for the duration, they have great energy at first. When there is doubt, or when they are challenged on their credibility or facts, liberal opponents will go on the attack (i.e., "When in doubt go on the attack"). Liberals have an aloofness, which has been described as a "distracted air," they go into action only when they have a crisis.
- Understand their Personality Style and use their own strategies and psyche against them.
- Remember the underlying quest of the liberal and liberal Democrat is that they want power, to be right, and in control, they do not like disagreement, and have a self-righteousness about their agendas, and they will not hesitate to skew facts or be devious to win an argument, an issue, or an election.

For example: During the writing of this book, I inadvertently sent pictures to a liberal relative from the *9/12 Project*, where Americans came by the tens-of-thousands to Washington D.C. to let the government know of their concerns about large budget deficit spending. I received a searing email complete with capitals to make emphasis. The relative culminated by referring to me as a *Republican racist bigot*. I was shocked by his explosive response, and his irreverence for fiscal responsibility and constitutional right to assemble, only to being bigoted and racist. In a return email I asked – Since when is the quest for fiscal responsibility racist? I have never received a response.

This is the reaction and rhetoric you can expect from the liberal left when they are faced with challenge or reality. They will always come back and accuse you of being insensitive, and of being a bigot and racist. These are their standard rebuttals.

The last thing people on the left want is to be challenged. Internally, the liberal psyche struggles with insecurity, envy, and over-focused sensitivity. These are breached when liberals are challenged with documented fact, detail, and reality. To them, being in power is about quenching these core desires and insecurities. Therefore, for them, big government is security.

Those on the left should not put everything into emotional and sensitivity responses. They need to first rationalize their data to determine if they are correct in their assumptions, otherwise they lose credibility. They also need to be willing to reach into their own pockets first, as the old saying goes, "Sweep your own door step first, before you sweep your neighbors."

Item 5 DNA - The Code Of Life, A Brief Overview
In human evolution, there are four basic DNA groups throughout the world from which we all came. Even though each of our natures is unique, all of us are 99 percent the same species. It is only the last one percent of the DNA molecule that makes us unique. What is ironic is that we are also 99 percent related to chimpanzees. However, even though we are all one species throughout the world, we have many different physical characteristics with the remaining one percent. Other than skin toning and facial characteristics, there are many examples. With vigorous physical activity our bodies sweat to keep cool. Africans sweat the most, then Caucasians, and last Asians when doing similar activity. Asians have more difficulty tolerating alcoholic spirits, the so-called *Asian flush* is a reaction to alcohol. Less pigmented skin developed in northern areas, whereas darker pigmented skin developed in warm sunny areas. Each race evolved based on the geographic and climate conditions of the area.

As time and research proceed, the DNA molecule will ultimately explain all our human condition and idiosyncrasies. We will understand scientifically the reasons for human thinking, in two predominant political spheres (liberal & conservative), the Personality Styles themselves, the underlying causes of conditions like Cancer, Alzheimer's, Autism, ADHD, AIDS, and the nature of intelligence, criminology, and sexual preference.

Genetics is the natural random selection which creates many possibilities. We as a species could have been asexual, a term referring to the ability to reproduce by one's self. That is, without a partner. Many plants are asexual, propagating by the individual plant (the flowers they create have both sets of sex organs contained within the same plant). Asexual reproduction recreates the species exactly. This is similar to cloning where the offspring is an identical reproduction of the first. This, however, can be detrimental to a species in the case of disease. If a blight occurs, it could destroy the whole species because each individual is identical to the other.

In sexual reproduction, chromosomes are randomly shared by both parents. This makes the offspring the same species, but uniquely different in their individual composition. This randomness protects against epidemics and diseases. Each individual has a slightly different DNA, so a disease may affect a great portion of the population, but there will still be some survivors because of the unique difference of each individual, assuring the continuation of the species. This slight difference is easily seen in families where comparison of characteristics to present and past family members reveals grandmother's brow line, Uncle Will's characteristic smile, Aunt Jane's brilliant blue eyes, etc.

Item 6 The United States Constitution Brief History
When beginning the process of independence the Congress of the Colonies had to first declare their independence from England and King George III. This they did with *THE DECLARATION OF INDEPENDENCE* written by Thomas Jefferson, which stated the colonies should be free and independent states. The declaration was completed July 2, 1776, and presented on July 4, 1776. Shortly thereafter, the Congress passed the Articles of Confederation, which was the first U.S. Constitution. It was written in precise language to avoid misinterpretation.

Under the Articles of Confederation there was weak national authority and no executive power to impose federal tax, control trade or enforce legislation. The loose confederation of autonomous states had many squabbles and disputes in Congress. States could not be compelled to honor national obligations. The new United States of America also owed its patriots over 42 million dollars (billions in today's dollars) from the Revolutionary War. It was difficult to resolve disputes over issues, especially taxes and interstate tariffs, and paying the bills incurred during the Revolution. The only way to resolve these issues was to have a strong central government. Therefore, a federal constitution needed to be designed which would improve upon the weaknesses inherent to the Articles of Confederation.

Initially the founding fathers were reluctant to have a strong centralized government because of the tyranny they had lived under from British rule. To have the states work together as a nation with centralized control, a federal constitution was adopted September 17, 1787. In 1789, under the new Federal Constitution, GEORGE WASHINGTON was elected the first President of the United States, by a vote of citizens. The Constitution was ratified with a Bill of Rights on December 15, 1791. Washington served two terms but refused a third term.

Outlined below is the Constitution under which we operate. It is referred to as the Federal Constitution, because it replaced the Articles of Confederation. The new Constitution gave power to the individual citizen as opposed to the Articles of Confederation, where power was given to individual states. Under the Articles, each state would form its own constitution under which it would function. Ironically, none of the language in either the Articles of Confederation, or the Federal Constitution forbids states to secede.

THE CONSTITUTION of THE UNITED STATES OF AMERICA
Preamble: *We the People of the United States, in Order to form a more perfect union, establish Justice, insure domestic tranquility, provide for the common defense, promote the general welfare, and secure the blessings of Liberty to ourselves and our Posterity, do ordain and establish this Constitution for the United States of America [Ratified June 1788].*

John Adams stated, "The American Constitution was only for the American people, for no other; and for the Republic to flourish, by the end of the day, there has to be a certain level of virtue in people."

Article 1 The Legislative Department
Article 2 The Executive Department
Article 3 The Judicial Department
Article 4 Relations between the States
Article 5 The Amendment Process
Article 6 General Provisions, Supremacy of Constitution
Article 7 Ratification of the Constitution

Original Bill of Rights (*the first ten amendments, ratified 1791*)
1. *Freedom of religion, speech, press, assembly, petition.*
2. *Militia and right to bear arms.*
3. *Quartering of troops (the British required Colonists to board their troops).*
4. *Unlawful searches and seizures.*
5. *Rights of accused persons.*
6. *The right to a speedy and public trial.*
7. *The right to trial by jury in common law cases.*
8. *Reasonable bail and punishment.*
9. *Protects rights that are not specifically mentioned in the Constitution, are still guaranteed to the people.*
10. *Powers not mentioned in the Constitution for federal government is reserved to the states.*

Later amendments
11. *Suits against states, 1795.*
12. *Elections of President and Vice-President, 1804.*
13. *Slavery was abolished, 1865.*
14. *Protections, privileges of citizens of states, 1868.*
15. *Voting rights of all races, 1870.*
16. *Income tax power granted to congress, 1913.*
17. *Election of senators by the people, 1913.*
18. *Prohibition of intoxicating beverages, 1919.*
19. *Right to vote guaranteed to both sexes, 1920.*
20. *"Lame Duck" session of congress eliminated, 1933.*
21. *Repeal of eighteenth amendment, rescinding prohibition, 1933.*
22. *Limit on President's term of office to two terms, 1951.*
23. *Voting rights for District of Columbia, 1961.*
24. *Prohibition on poll tax, 1964.*
25. *Provision for disability of President, 1967.*
26. *Voting age of eighteen, 1971.*
27. *Senator & Representative compensation, 1992.*

Item 7 Brief History of the Evolution of Federal Taxes[4]

Federal taxation has been an evolving process through our nation's history. At first, because of the Articles of Confederation, where colonies (states) had individual power, the federal government had limited need for tax revenue. The federal government would receive operating funds from the colonies. In the south, colonies taxed imports and exports for revenue. The middle colonies imposed property tax or "poll tax" on each male adult. In New England revenue was raised with real estate taxes, excise taxes and occupation taxes (similar to the middle colonies). After the new Federal Constitution was enacted in 1789, which gave power to the Federal government, federal tax revenue came from excise taxes, tariffs, and customs duties.

Ironically, imposition of taxes by England is one of the sparks that ultimately made us a free nation. At that time in history, England was at war with France and needed more revenue. By 1765 England passed the "Stamp Act" the first tax imposed on the colonies. Then they put a tax on tea. Since the colonies had no representation, they were forced to pay these taxes, hence the cry, "Taxation without representation is tyranny." This began the process of American independence with the Revolutionary War. To pay for the war, Congress levied taxes on liquor, tobacco and snuff, refined sugar, carriages, property sold at auctions, and certain legal documents. Over 200 years later, during the writing of this book, tobacco and liquor are still enduring high taxation (those who do not approve of distilled spirits and tobacco, feel it proper to impose high taxes on these items out of moral conscience to quell their use). For over 200 years this has been a societal denial of individual choice.

These early taxes did not attempt to equalize incomes or wealth, or the ideology of redistribution of wealth; as is inherent in today's liberal left. After their experience with England, Americans continued to resist taxes that seemed unfair, too high, or improper. The first "direct tax" (i.e. a reoccurring tax directly from the taxpayer to the federal government based on the value of an item) was imposed in the 1790s on owners of houses, land, and slaves to help pay for the skirmishes with the French during this time. With his election in 1802, Thomas Jefferson abolished direct taxes. But by the time of the War of 1812, Congress imposed additional excise taxes, specific customs duties, and by issuing Treasury Notes to fund the war. In 1817 these taxes were repealed, and for 44 years the federal government received most of its revenue from customs duties and through the sale of public land. Prior to 1913, taxes were considered only to be instituted for emergency, such as in time of war. It was the expectation that these enacted taxes would be rescinded after the national emergency.

At the beginning of the Civil War, the Revenue Act of 1861 was enacted, which restored earlier excise taxes and a three percent tax on personal incomes above $800 per year. This is the first time in our nation's history that a "personal income tax" was imposed on citizens. Because of growing war debt, on July 1, 1862 Congress passed new excise taxes on playing cards, gunpowder, feathers, telegrams, iron, leather, pianos, yachts, billiard tables, drugs, patent medicines, whiskey, and on legal documents, and license fees were collected for professions and trades. The 1862 tax reform established a two-tier rate structure. Incomes up to $10,000 were taxed at three percent, and higher incomes taxed at five percent. An annual deduction of $600 was enacted with deductions allowed for rental housing, repairs, losses, and other taxes paid. Taxes were also "withheld at the source" by employers, so government received on-going and timely revenue.

After the war, less federal revenue was required to run the government and most taxes were repealed with ongoing taxation on tobacco and liquor. The Income Tax was abolished in 1872, with excise tax revenue and tariffs supporting the government until 1913. Finding these forms of taxation unreliable and unbalanced, a constitutional amendment was initiated to impose a tax on businesses and individual incomes. President Wilson signed into law the 16th amendment to the Constitution on October 3, 1913, which made federal taxation into law. It read, "Congress shall have the power to lay and collect taxes on incomes, from whatever source derived without apportionment among the several states and without regard to any census, or enumeration." Rates from one percent to seven percent were established based on income level. However, less than one percent of the population actually paid taxes at the time. Aware of the new invasion of government into the internal affairs of business and family incomes, the government gave protection by making information from tax returns confidential.

After World War One, as tax rates declined, the economy was strengthened. This is what caused the economic era referred to as the "Roaring Twenties", until October 1929 when the stock market crash occurred. Wars have always required additional revenue collection. Good economy increases the collection of federal taxes. When business and the free market do well, revenue to the government does well, but during down economic times the government receives less revenue. During these times, lowering taxes generally stimulates the economy to grow; therefore, increasing federal and state revenue. But during the Great Depression, Congress enacted the Tax Act of 1932 which increased tax rates, this was followed by another drastic tax increase in 1936 (4–79 percent rate), then in 1940 two additional tax laws increased individual and corporate taxes, followed with another tax increase in 1941. In 1935 the Social Security Act mandated payments called, "Unemployment Compensation," providing compensation to those who lost their jobs, gave public aid to the aged, needy, and handicapped. This was originally financed by a two percent tax, one-half taken directly from an employee's paycheck, and the other half from the employer. The tax was levied on the first $3,000 of income. These rates have continued to increase over time.

All these increases weakened the economy, which prolonged the Great Depression. Only World War Two and its need for production finally pulled America out of the depression. In 1941, again because of the need for timely cash flow during the war, the government began withholding taxes from individual paychecks. Therefore, employees only received net paychecks after these taxes. When this was enacted, Congress again promised to rescind it after the war. But, unlike when this direct method of tax collection was repealed after the Civil War, and the First World War, it was never repealed after World War Two, and continues today. Both the Tax Reform Act of 1969 and the Economic Recovery Tax Act of 1981, both by Republican administrations, helped reduce individual tax burden. The 1981 Economic Recovery Act also instituted the Individual Retirement Account (IRA).

Now you know why taxation has been such an issue throughout our history. Taxes continued as a way of life for Americans. We have always paid our share, but as society has moved more and more to the left, more taxes are asked for nonessential and nontraditional reasons, burdening those that pay taxes. Taxes erode a family income and budget, quell entrepreneurship and the will to produce, and therefore, the economy. Without good economy the government has less tax revenues to operate on. This is why there is public outcry to keep the size of government under control and as efficient as possible.

The most important thing to remember as a tax paying citizen is that since the pre-collection of taxes was never rescinded after World War Two, and probably never will be, the government has greatly reduced the taxpayer's awareness of the amount of taxes actually being collected, and how much less your income really is. The government has made the payment of taxes less obvious, and is, therefore, much easier for government to raise future taxes on the populous. Remember what Thomas Jefferson said, "A government big enough to give you everything you want, is strong enough to take everything you have."

Item 8 Representation
One persons view on representation
It is important to understand the lousy representation we have as citizens. Our representatives do not base their votes or judgment on what we wish as citizens, and consistently make aberrations to the United States Constitution, which they should be upholding. This was obvious during the unpopular 2010 national healthcare debate, when over 100,000 phone calls an hour were coming into Washington D.C., requesting that the bill not be passed. But incumbents did not listen to their constituents and voted for the unpopular and poorly orchestrated bill anyway. Most legislators did not even know what the bill contained, nor did they take the time to find out. In her poorly thought out immortal phrase, Nancy Pelosi voiced, "We have to pass the bill so that you [representatives] can find out what's in it."

The majority of the American population was against the healthcare bill, especially in its convoluted development, to be passed. They spoke, but the government did not listen. These are the depths to where our elected representatives have gone. No wonder Americans are angry with Congress, our president, and the government in general. Thomas Jefferson referred to this as tyranny.

The following is a response from a long-time family friend who spent time in the state legislature, his view on legislation:

"After serving for eight sessions at the State Legislature, here are a few classifications I have for legislators: 1) Too dumb to represent the people that elected them, 2) Those pursuing their particular personal desire, 3) Those that are satisfying the pressures of powerful lobbyists, and, 4) Those that take the time to discuss a problem or bill with knowledgeable people at the citizen level."

I suspect this could be magnified to the national level and be a fairly accurate model of federal representation.

President Harry S. Truman should be a great example to all elected officials
The only asset Mr. Truman had when he died was his house in Independence, Missouri in which he lived. His wife had inherited the house from her mother. When President Truman retired from office in 1952 he relied on an income of $13,507 from an army pension. When Congress was informed that Mr. Truman was paying for his own postage stamps to answer the correspondence he received, they granted him an allowance and retroactive pension of $25,000 per annum.

President Truman and his wife, Bess, drove themselves to attend President Eisenhower's inauguration, with no secret service protection. When Truman was offered corporate positions with a good salary, he declined and stated, "You don't want me. You want the office of the President, and that doesn't belong to me. It belongs to the American people and it's not for sale." As president, he paid for all his own travel expenses and food.

In his later years, when Congress was going to award him the Medal of Honor on his 87th birthday, President Truman refused the award writing, "I don't consider that I have done anything which should be the reason for any award, Congressional or otherwise." These were before the days when Presidents established libraries to honor themselves.

Known to use the full gamut of the English language, President Truman once summarized his choice in life, "My choices in life were either to be a piano player in a whore house or a politician. And to tell the truth, there's hardly any difference."

Should our modern presidents capture even one percent of President Truman's humility and honesty, we would be a better nation.

Item 9 The 2008 Campaign

The campaign separated the left from the right, and showed the anger the populous has had pent up against government. With Congress having record lows in approval, and forty years of sliding to the left, it had taken a toll on the populous, and their frustration was released during this election.

Even with an unpopular war, and economic tragedies occurring in the housing market simultaneously with the election, almost 50 percent of the nation was still reluctant to just vote Democrat. People were unsure of its first time black president, not because of color, but because of his unsavory affiliations and reluctance to release any tangible information about himself. The reverse also occurred. Much party-jumping occurred, and cross-over votes, as America was trying to understand what was really going on. Since it was a black candidate running for the first time for president, the majority of the Black community committed their vote to Obama, regardless of his questionable affiliations.

Many could not separate themselves from the last eight years of George W. Bush and the Iraq War to vote for Republican John McCain, even though McCain touted himself as his own person. Added to this hype was the determination of the Democrats to be in power since their party had been out for the last eight years, and many still felt the contested election of 2000 should have been theirs. Ideologically it was like the Civil War, brother against brother, cousin against cousin, generation against generation.

While listening to a talk radio station during the campaign, a listener called in who worked for the FBI. He pointed out that with the questionable affiliations that Mr. Obama had in his personal life, that Mr. Obama would not be hired by the FBI. Instead, he ran for president of the United States and was elected.

Letter to Chicago Tribune During the 2008 Election
Given my childhood, I could not help but write a letter to the editor of the Chicago Tribune during the McCain-Obama election, when I heard Michelle Obama's explanation of being poor, as having only one bathroom. This shows how our society has been consistently improving and how poverty has been redifined. If you cannot afford designer clothing, or live in a dwelling with only one bathroom, you are poor. This has given poverty a new, higher level. It is also ironic that even the poorest in our nation are overweight. Do we truly have poor people in this nation? Do we really know what it means to be poor?

The following letter was sent to the Chicago Tribune, in response to Michelle Obama's mention of being raised in poverty during the primary election.[5]

"I can truly say that I am not happy with any of the candidates for President of the United States of America. It is the most powerful position in the world and we seem to take it for granted. We do not seem to have high quality people seek the position, only self-fulfilling individuals with their own agendas.

What finally prompted this letter was the recent interview of Michelle Obama on national television. She told of how she grew up on the Southside of Chicago. It was tragic that her father had MS. But she went on to say that she was raised in a one-bedroom, one-bathroom apartment. I thought, well how does that make you really poor?

I will explain to you what real poverty is. I was born in 1950 in a small town in northern Minnesota. We rented the main level of a condemned house at the edge of town, built in 1890. It had straw insulation and was a tinderbox, which is why the city condemned it. I was dragged from my bed while growing up because of one of many chimney fires. I remember being held in my mother's arms, a blanket wrapped around me in the middle of a cold winter night, watching flames a foot or more shoot out of our chimney. Only a few short years after we moved, the city burnt it down as a practice for their volunteer fire department.

The house only had cold water coming into it, but no indoor plumbing, which meant you had to empty the "slop-pail" under the sink. The sink was set in a wood frame with a curtain hiding the slop-pail. Many times this five-gallon pail would run over before we realized it was full and needed to be emptied. Since we did not have plumbing we used an outhouse. But during the winter and at night, we had to use an indoor pot which had to be emptied daily into the outhouse. I had this dubious task on many occasions after my grown sisters left home.

We only had a kerosene space heater in the middle of the living room, so during the winter months, my parents closed up the adjacent bedrooms and we all slept in the one open living room and kitchen. That way, we could all benefit from the single heat source. I remember one time my mother gave me the only money she had, a fifty-cent piece, and told me to take the empty kerosene can and go get some fuel for the heater. A gas station was about a block away if you cut through neighbor's yards. I used my sled to bring the kerosene home.

We eventually moved to the Twin Cities when I was ten years old. It was the last opportunity for my parents, at their age, to still try to make good. It was the first time in my life that I had a "flush toilet" in a one-bedroom apartment that we all shared. But the apartment was warm, had indoor plumbing, and a stove that never needed a gas tank to be periodically replaced, as we had to do with our stove back home.

I eventually worked my way through public school and paid my way through college by working part-time. I remember that I would walk ten blocks to my classes every day so that I would not have to pay a parking meter. My two sisters also worked their way through school. I can honestly say that we are all self-made. Everything that I had, I had bought and paid for by my honest labor and budgeting of money. My parents could not co-sign for me for an automobile because they did not have good credit and my father had bouts with alcoholism.

I thought I would share my experience. It can still be done -- you only have to want to do it. You must still believe in yourself and your individual freedom of choice. We have moved away from our pioneer spirit and now expect government to fulfill our every whim. This has eroded our society and our individual spirit. It was difficult for me to hear Michelle Obama say how poor she was, when I thought I was the richest person on earth when we moved into our apartment in the city that had a "flush toilet" and steady heat, with a stove that did not need gas-cylinders to be replaced."

Letter concerning the Norm Coleman and Al Franken Senate race
The following letter was sent to the St. Paul Pioneer Press:

"By now the nation is familiar with the close senate race, and subsequent court battles in Minnesota between Norm Coleman and Al Franken. As a life-long Minnesotan, I can assure you that Norm Coleman is the better person. A relative has personally worked with him while he was mayor of St. Paul. Mr. Coleman did a lot of positive things for St. Paul and the St. Paul School District, and for the State of Minnesota as a Senator.

I feel it is the bias media that is labeling Mr. Coleman as the bad guy. People across the nation need to understand from a Minnesota view, not from the biased media. On the other hand, you have Al Franken who has never held an elected position, has been out of the State of Minnesota for thirty years, and is known nationally as a hard leftist liberal. How is he going to be beneficial to the State of Minnesota? He was placed here by the Democratic National Committee (DNC) only to win another seat.

It is ironic to note when Franken was behind Coleman in the original final election count, how one voting volunteer just happened to find an additional number of ballots in his trunk that he had "forgotten about", and ironically they were all for Democrat Al Franken. This brought a moment of humor even in the media. The younger vote is who put Franken in, and it was only because of his connection to *Saturday Night Live* did they know of him.

I think it is good that Norm Coleman is pursuing his course of action, bringing his case before the State Court, and if need be to the Supreme Court. It will establish precedence for the future as these things reoccur; as they did with the Bush-Gore election on a national level. I question how is Al Franken going to improve our state when his extreme liberal stance is only representative of the hard left?"

Item 10 Too Much Sensitivity & The Housing Collapse

The housing collapse was a prime example of oversensitivity with little forethought for future outcome, it came full circle to plague the masses and global economy. You do not build a strong America by giving away credit responsibility. Janet Reno, the Attorney General under the Clinton Administration, utilized the Community Reinvestment Act to pressure banks into giving loans to those with little ability to pay them back. She vowed she would bring legal action against banks and institutions that in her judgment, refused minorities and persons of limited means, to purchase a house. In her vernacular, discrimination had a broad context. In other words, do not turn down a minority even if it seems wise to do so, based on their financial capability. With the paranoia and disdain the left has for business, and since the Attorney General had no banking or practical finance experience, her opinion was that these banks were racist. This intimidation was reinforced by the questionable practices of groups such as ACORN, who intimidated banks and institutions that much more. In essence, this began the initial step to the ultimate crash of the housing industry.

How can a bank refuse a home buyer, without the necessary credit and funds and the ability to repay, when you are constantly being called racist and prodded by groups such as ACORN? Banks began refusing fewer applications from persons of limited means, especially from minorities, who were unable to qualify for housing loans.

Banks would write the loan, then sell it as soon as possible to the government sponsored enterprises *Fannie Mae and Freddie Mac*.[6] Banks treated the worthless loan paperwork as a hot potato to be gotten rid of as soon as possible. These worthless bundles of paper, in turn, were repackaged by overzealous brokers as investment grade securities, which were purchased the world over. These high-risk contracts kept piling up at Fannie Mae and Freddie Mac to over a trillion dollars. This liberal oversensitivity without regard for consequences, through the Attorney General's edit, prompted the beginning of the housing collapse.

Most of these housing contracts were written as an ARM (Adjustable Rate Mortgage), one small way the banks could protect themselves. With relaxed loan qualifications, a home could be sold to almost anyone. As trends with housing have always gone, when interest rates are low, prices for real estate inflate. "Home ownership did increase from 64 percent, the average of the previous 35 years before 1995, to 69 percent by 2004."[7] But, "By the end of 2007, more than 17 percent of subprime borrowers had fallen behind on their loan payments."[7] Then young, upstart Wall Street brokers took these poor loans and converted them into triple-A bonds to camouflage their value, grouped them into Ordinary Participation Certificates (CPOs), and sold them abroad. China became a large benefactor of these over-rated investments.

Rising home prices with low interest rates, and low or no payments down, along with sub-prime rates with ARMs made the housing market explode. But with strong growth, easy profits and commissions, greed got into the formula. More and more development was occurring farther and farther from city centers as gasoline prices continued to increase. By the year 2006, the housing market was showing signs of stress. One indicator that should have been obvious is that house prices were steadily increasing while wages were not. This created an unstable disparity. Because of rampant growth of the housing market, the chairman of the Federal Reserve thought it wise to slow the momentum, so he proposed a slight adjustment in the interest rate. Barely a decade after Janet Reno began to heavy hand the banks, which caused them to write loans to those who could not afford a house, it all came down in ruin. Almost overnight the housing market imploded in upon itself. Ironically, the crash occurred during a presidential election.

Because of growing concerns about the overheated housing market, regulatory reform was presented by the Bush Administration in 2005,[8] but it was not acted upon with any serious consideration by Congress. The sitting president had pre-warned congress about impending housing concerns on other occasions throughout his two terms, but it was not considered an urgent matter. "Current House Banking Committee chairman Rep. Barney Frank of Massachusetts opposed legislation to reorganize oversight in 2000 (when Clinton was still president), 2003 and 2004, saying of the 2000 legislation that concern about Fannie and Freddie was 'overblown.'"[9] Just before the election of 2008,"Senate Banking Committee chairman Chris Dodd called a Bush proposal for an independent agency to regulate the two entities "ill-advised."[9]

Overall, there was poor oversight both by federal government and the Securities and Exchange Commission (SEC). One person put it in perspective, "Never attribute to corporate malice what can be explained by poorly thought out regulation." The housing crisis was a major example of liberal short-sightedness from the get-go that came full circle and caused world financial and social scorn. This is why we must take our society out of liberal gridlock and move it back to center. Otherwise, these events will be repeated again and again because of short-sighted decisions based on oversensitivity. This housing crisis took barely a decade to come full circle. Unfortunately, the Obama Administration chose the route of expanded government and increased national debt to try and solve the problem.

The concern is, with the events occurring during the writing of this book (historical large government bailouts), that the federal government will continue to help individuals who have not made the best choices, and corporations that have not remained competitive and efficient enough to persist. This will cause other major fall-outs in the future. Considering the housing collapse, many responsible citizens have asked if it is fair, that millions of Americans who borrowed more than they could afford, are now being bailed out by the government to stave off foreclosure. A liberal government and society continues to reward failure and poor judgment, which sends the message that it is OK if I make poor decisions or default, because I will get bailed out.

Item 11 The Day America Stood Still
In a time beyond, with decades of criticism, blame, and taxation, the environment had become hostile to those on the conservative side of the political spectrum. They found themselves scapegoats and realized it better to move on. Overnight they left America with what they had been able to save and what little wealth they had left. They took their businesses and corporations with them in hope of a better life elsewhere.

They spread their dollars and entrepreneurship in other lands, where they could flourish and be an appreciated part of the society. They were leaving a society that had ultimately become their master and was choking them with taxation, socialism, eroded social culture, and lack of respect for individual freedoms and enterprise. Capitalists, conservatives, and Republicans had to move on because their environment had been drastically changed and they became concerned for their safety. Raging liberalist and socialist dogma had suppressed freedoms and free enterprise, and government had grown to a dictatorial omnipresence. There had been unabated continuous growth in government and government sponsored programs.

Since government had already forced its hand into many private industries, elected officials were unconcerned with the exit of the capitalists and business owners. In fact the exodus was heralded as a win for liberal ideology and socialist gain.

The religious principles that were part of the founding of America were no longer obvious in the society. They had been replaced with abridged freedoms and government expectations. The socialist government attempted to show the rest of the world how productive this new society was through displays of science and art. To show how it was progressing without the burden of the greedy capitalist culture.

The media, which was always used to taking the side of the left, had to work full-time to rationalize that things would improve, especially now since the greedy capitalists were gone. The media, however, continued to blame the conservatives and capitalists even long after they were gone for the ever growing problems of supply and demand, and the poor national economy. The media summarized it as the tentacles of the "culture of greed" reaching back still to cause problems.

The populous became ever more complacent and needed the constant prod of government sponsored media ads just to be motivated to show up for work. It had been instilled in citizens that government should be your constant companion and solve all your concerns.

Waiting lists and lines begin to form for various products, such as toilet tissue and fresh meat and produce. These were only available on select days. Disgruntled persons were forced to stand in line. Some questioned what had happened, but were not heard, as the expanding socialist government stifled their concerns, personal liberties, and the society.

Those in control were in appointed and nepotistic positions and became the elite in their own right, having free rein in politics, persuasion, and amenities. But it still did not afford them the lifestyle to which they were accustomed under a free market capitalist environment. The government was weighed heavy with entitlement and socialist promises but did not have the tax base to fulfill its wishes. Without the ready resources of the capitalist faction of society, its entrepreneurism was no longer available to be tapped from. But those in elected positions continued to promise that everything would right itself.

Since the government had relied on 45 percent or more of taxes from individuals, its base and budget had become drastically reduced, and many people were without jobs because the capitalists that had created them left the country. They had reestablished themselves elsewhere where they continued their free market entrepreneurship, and building a better life. This caused not only a problem for the present, but for the foreseeable future. There had been a vacuum created by this exodus of former business owners, employers, and the former free market society, with the reality that the remaining needs of federal revenue had always been obtained from taxes on businesses.

The federal government created large budget deficits because of the lack of a steady diet of taxes. The persons remaining in society were of liberal conscience; therefore, more used to bringing all their problems and concerns to government to be solved. Because of the deteriorating circumstances, government could no longer uphold its budget and, therefore, its programs and promises. As might be expected, this caused chaos throughout the land, and the overtly outspoken socialist-populous threatened riot. But against whom? Their frustration had to be channeled, so again they blamed the capitalists for letting them down, and for leaving them in such a situation.

It became a culture of despair and anarchy as those used to the protective veil of government funds became destitute and resorted to supplying their needs however they could. Those at the top of the political spectrum did not suffer nearly as bad. They were first in line for necessities and the luxuries of life. Their elitist positions dictated so.

They say history repeats itself, especially if people do not read history -- and that was the case here.

NOTES

Chapter Two

1. It is difficult to conceive how much a trillion really is (one trillion = 1,000,000,000,000). Few calculators go to that many digits. Do the math; there are 31,536,000 seconds in a year, if we were to go back in time one-trillion seconds it would be over 31,709 years ago! A trillion is a very large amount!
2. A phrase penned by John F. Kennedy, but taken from Justice Oliver Wendell Homes, Jr., to be included in Kennedy's inaugural address written by Ted Sorenson, JFK's special counsel, advisor, and primary speech writer. Sorenson was also the ghost writer for the book "Profiles of Courage" by John F. Kennedy.

Chapter three

1. Source: Newsmax.com/insidecover/ Wayne_root_radio_show/2009.
2. Source: www.wikipedia.org/wiki/Toba_catastrophe_theory.
3. Source: www.vulcan.wr.usgs.gov/volcanos/iceland.
4. Source: www.ncdc.noaa.gov/paleo/globalwarming/medieval.html.
5. Source: www.crh.noaa.gov/mqt/?n=lake_superior_ice; and, http://climate. umn.edu/doc/jounal/superior 030603.html.
6. Source: www.nasa.gov/worldbook/mars_worldbook_prt.htm.
7. Source: Newsmax.com on-line; Scientist: Global Warming Claims a Lot of Hype (July 3, 2009).
8. Source: www.history.com (The Discovery Channel).
9. Source: www.census.gov/Press-Release/www/releases/archives/education (2007).
10. Source: Yoel Inbar, Cornell University, Department of Psychology, Ithaca, New York.

Chapter Six

1. Sources: www.house.gov; www.senate.gov; www.thecapitol.net/FAQ/ payandperqs.htm.
2. Source: www.usgovinfo.about.com/od/uscongress/a/congresspay.htm (2009). As of October 1, 2006 there were 413 retired members of congress; 290 receive an average of $60,972 (x 290 = $17,681,880), and123 members receive an average of $35,952 (x 123 = $4,422,096); a total of $22,103,976.
3. Source: Citizens Against Government Waste (www.cagw.org).
4. "OUR ENDANGERED VALUES America's Moral Crisis" by Jimmy Carter, Simon & Schuster, New York, ISBN 978-0-7432-8457-8.

Chapter Eight

1. The Chronicle of Higher Education (www.chronicle.com), reports each year how professors describe themselves politically.

Chapter Nine
1. Source: www.wisconsinhistory.org/turningpoints/tp-035 (Robert M. LaFollette).
2. Source: www.archives/gov/federal-register/electoral-college/faq.html.
3. The Electoral College by William C. Kimberling, Deputy Director FEC Office of Election Administration (Revised May 1992)

Chapter Twelve
1. Source: www.legislature.ne.gov/history_unicameral (Nebraska unicameral state government).

Appendix
1. Source: Jefferson Lab (www.jlab.org/div_dept/train/rad_guide/effects.html; 2008).
2. Source: www.cfo.doe.gov/me70/manhattan/hiroshima.htm.
3. The National Academies, Health Effects of Radiation; Radiation Effects Research Foundation (www.rerf.jp)
4. Source: www.tax.org/museum, and, www.ustres.gov/education.
5. To my knowledge, this letter to the editor was never published by the Chicago Tribune, I assume because of the political nature of the article during the election.
6. Fannie Mae, Federal National Mortgage Association (FNMA), a government sponsored enterprise (GSE) founded in 1938, and chartered by Congress in 1968 into a private shareholder-owned corporation. These GSE's operate in the secondary mortgage market, funding mortgages by issuing debt securities in domestic and international markets. Freddie Mac, Federal Home Loan Mortgage Corporation (FHFA) was established by Congress in 1970.
7. Source: The Heritage Foundation, www.heritage.org/research/economy.
8. The Federal Housing Enterprise Regulatory Reform Act of 2005 would have established a single regulatory entity over Fannie Mae and Freddie Mac.
9. Source: www.factcheck.org/elections-2008/who_caused_the_economic_crisis.

Some Resources to be Familiar With

AMERICAN ASSOCIATION OF RETIRED PERSONS (AARP)
www.aarp.org.
A liberal orientated interest group for retired people age 50 and over in the United States. Mission statement, "AARP is dedicated to enhancing quality of life for all as we age. We lead positive social change and deliver value to members through information, advocacy and service." A similar and newer organization, with more conservative leaning is the Association of Mature American Citizens (AMAC).

AMERICAN CIVIL LIBERTIES UNIION (ACLU)
www.aclu.org.
A liberal orientated interest group in the United States. It has brought up legislation that has ruled against such things as displaying signs that say, "In God We Trust."

AMERICAN LEGISLATIVE EXCHANGE COUNCIL (ALEC)
Washington D.C.,
www.alec.org.
A nonpartisan association for conservative state lawmakers who share common beliefs in limited government, free markets, federalism, and individual liberty, founded in 1973.

AMERICAN MAJORITY, Purcellville, Virginia
www.americanmajority.org.
A nonprofit, nondenominational organization that trains persons who wish to go into public office or to become community activists. Their goal is to build a national network of leaders and grass roots advocates who are dedicated to individual freedom and freedom in the marketplace. They believe that change begins at the state and local grassroots level.

ASSOCIATION OF COMMUNITY ORGANIZATIONS FOR REFORM NOW (ACORN)
www.acorn.org.
Founded in 1970, ACORN's original goal was to help people with housing, health care, immigration concerns, and registering voters. It became a very left organization with questionable practices, especially regarding voter fraud. It is organized as a shell with over 200 separate organizations functioning within it, many claiming to be charities and thus seeking government funding.

ASSOCIATION OF MATURE AMERICAN CITIZENS (AMAC),
Bohemia, New York
info@amac.us.
AMAC is a counterpart to AARP but believes in more conservative principles and values. It provides information, auto and house insurance, services, and retail discounts for members.

CITIZENS AGAINST GOVERNMENT WASTE, Washington, D.C.
www.cagw.org.
A taxpayer watchdog organization and source for earmark "Pork Barrel" spending, since 1991 has published the annual Congressional Pig Book acknowledging a list of Pork Barrel projects in federal government.

CITIZENS COUNCIL ON HEALTH FREEDOM, St. Paul, Minnesota
www.cchfreedom.org.
CCHC is concerned with newborn rights and genetic privacy laws. At the writing of this book there were 815,000 samples of baby DNA in warehouses (HIPA 600,000 entries). This is happening to 200 babies a day. The project initially began July 1, 1986 and the taking of baby DNA begin in 1997. Once you sign a HIPA form, they can share your data with anyone.

DEPARMENT OF HOMELAND SECURITY, Washington, D.C.
www.dhs.gov.
An umbrella organization of United States government agencies instituted in 2003 in response to the September 11, 2001 terrorist attack.

DRUDGE REPORT
www.drudgereport.com.
A conservative news website maintained by Matt Drudge and Andrew Breitbart. The website is a link to stories from the US and international news media concerning politics and current events. It was founded in 1997 and was the first news source to report the Monica Lewinski scandal to the public. Newsweek had decided not to publish the story.

FACTCHECK.ORG, University of Pennsylvania
www.FactCheck.org.
A nonpartisan and nonprofit project of the Annenberg Public Policy Center of the University of Pennsylvania. Instituted to be a resource and advocate helping to reduce the level of deception and confusion in U.S. politics for voters.

JOHN BIRCH SOCIETY, Appleton, WI
www.jbs.org.
Founded in 1958 by Robert Welch and is dedicated to restoring and preserving freedom under the United States Constitution. Active in all states on local, regional and national levels, it maintains a strong belief in personal freedom and limited government.

JUDICIAL WATCH Inc.
www.judicialwatch.org.
A conservative, nonpartisan educational foundation promoting integrity, transparency and accountability in government, politics, and the law. It advocates high standards and ethics in our elected officials and in our society.

MANHATTAN INSTITUTE FOR POLICY RESEARCH,
New York, N.Y.
www.manhatten-institute.org.
A conservative based think-tank founded by William J. Casey in 1978, with the mission to develop and disseminate ideas that create greater economic choices and individual responsibility. Mr. Casey later became President Ronald Reagan's CIA Director.

NATIONAL RIGHT TO WORK Legal Defense Foundation
www.nrtw.org.
Supports the right of employees to decide for themselves whether or not to join or financially support a union. Defends American workers from compulsory unionism. Employees who work in the railway or airline industries, and some federal areas are not protected by Right to Work Laws. Established in 1968.

NATIONAL TAXPAYERS UNION, Alexandria, Virginia
www.ntu.org.
A nonprofit, nonpartisan advocate for taxpayers founded in 1969. The organization is committed to tax relief and reform, lower and less wasteful government spending, individual liberty, and free enterprise. It believes Americans need major tax reform to make the tax system fair and uncomplicated.

POLITICO, Arlington, Virginia
www.politico.com.
Covers political news with focus on national politics, Congress, and Capitol Hill, the President, lobbying, and advocacy.

THE CATO INSTITUTE, Washington D.C.
www.cato.org.
A nonprofit public policy research foundation founded in 1977. Its mission is to increase the understanding of public policies based on the principles of limited government, free markets, and individual liberty.

THE INSTITUTE FOR JUSTICE, Arlington, Virginia
www.ij.org.
A nonprofit government watchdog headquartered in Washington D.C. They provide legal advice and representation, especially with local government since there are fewer checks and balances in local levels of government. Its core ideals: school choice, free speech, economic liberty, and property rights. Founded in 1991.

THE HERITAGE FOUNDATION, Washington, D.C.
www.heritage.org.
A conservative American think tank with the mission statement: "Formulate and promote conservative public policies based on the principles of free enterprise, limited government, individual freedom, traditional American values, and a strong national defense." Founded in 1973.

THE HEARTLAND INSTITUTE
www.heartland.org.
A nonprofit research and education organization not affiliated with any political party, business, or foundation. Their mission is to discover, develop, and promote free market solutions to social and economic problems. Such solutions include parental choice in education, personal responsibility in health care, market-based approaches to environmental protection, privatization of public services, and deregulation in areas where property rights and markets do a better job than government bureaucracies. Heartland does not accept government funds and does not conduct "contract" research for special interest groups.

REPUBLICAN NATIONAL LAWYERS ASSOCIATION (RNLA), Washington, D.C.
www.rnla.org.
Their mission is to advance the professionalism, education, and career opportunities of lawyers in political, government, legislative, and private firm settings. It seeks to promote open, fair, and honest elections at all levels of American society.

TAX FOUNDATION, Washington, D.C.
www.taxfoundation.org.
A nonpartisan tax education organization with the mission to educate taxpayers about tax policy and tax burden borne by Americans and government finance. Founded in 1937, the organization is independent in gathering information, and relies on voluntary contributions from business and individuals.

U.S. CHAMBER OF COMMERCE (USCC) Washington, D.C.
www.uschamber.com.
National nonprofit lobbying group representing many businesses and associations across the USA staffed with policy specialists, lobbyists, and lawyers. Founded in 1912.

UNITED STATES DEPARTMENT OF LABOR Occupational Safety and Health Administration (OSHA), Washington, D.C.
www.osha.gov.
Created by Congress in 1970.

UNITED STATES JUSTICE FOUNDATION (USJF), Ramona, California
usjf@usjf.net.
A nonprofit legal action organization founded in 1979 to inform, educate and litigate on significant legal issues. It also submits testimony to the U. S. Senate on Supreme Court appointees and other important legal issues. The foundation publishes and distributes materials to government officials and the public and also contributes to legal defense in specific cases.

WATCH DOG.ORG
www.watchdog.org.
A collection of independent journalists who cover state-specific and local government activity. The combined project involves investigative journalists to present their material, and reporters nationwide to share information, techniques and resources. Its purpose is to promote communication between journalists which in turn will create a better informed electorate and more transparent government. This group was founded in 2009.

D E F I N I T I O N S
FOR VARIOUS TERMS USED IN THIS WRITING

ANARCHY – The absence of political and social order. Lacking government, or an ineffectual governing body. A political entity which lacks a ruler or government causing lawlessness and disorder.

AUTHORITARIAN – A government structure where the dictator or a party monopolize political power. Authoritarian regimes control the state.

BOLSHEVIKS (Russian, majority) - Members of the Marxist-Leninist party that came to power during the Russian Revolution of 1917. The party goal was to seize national power and establish a communist form of government. This party became the Russian Communist Party.

CAPITALISM - A free market system with emphasis on productivity and profit geared toward the individual consumer.

CENTRISM (CENTRIST) – Political ideology promoting moderate policies which remain in the middle politically away from each extreme.

CIVIL RIGHTS – Personal human rights recognized and guaranteed by the United States Constitution.

COMMUNISM – A political-social system in which property and the means of production are held in common. A movement that wishes to overthrow capitalism by revolutionary means, and then establish a classless society in which all goods are owned in common. The original theory came from Karl Marx and was modified by Lenin. Socialism seeks the same result through evolution, instead of revolution. (See Socialism)

CONSERVATIVE – A person who adheres to principles of limited government, personal responsibility, and moral values. In the United States conservatives also believe in free market enterprise and support established institutions with limited government control.

DEMOCRACY – Government by the people, usually directly and through elected representatives. Rule by the majority. Democracy was never used in the Declaration of Independence or the Constitution. This is because a true democracy could never exist for any period of time without an overriding constitution. The term Democracy saw growth in its use about the 1930's and is associated with the administration of President Franklin D. Roosevelt. Its common usage today has evolved into many variations mainly concerned with masses and government by the majority.

DEMOCRATIC PARTY (DEMOCRAT) – One of two major parties in the United States. Its base is center-left from liberal Democrat to moderate Democrat. Democrats favor large government, taxation, regulation of business, and higher government spending. The Democrat Party has strong ties to organized labor and teacher unions.

DICTATORSHIP – An autocratic form of government ruled by an individual. A dictatorship is usually totalitarian in its nature. (See Authoritarian)

DOGMA – The established belief that is not to be challenged or diverged from, of a religion, political entity, or ideology. Dogma refers to the core principles that must be upheld by all members of the group. The term is usually in negative context

EARMARK (spending) – Any member of congress can request funding for a project, no matter what project. How earmarks are determined tend to fall on seniority (senatorial longevity), committee membership, and party affiliation. Earmarks are referred to as "Pork Barrel" projects because of their nonessential nature. At the writing of this book there was little accountability for controlling earmarks, and members of congress are not required to disclose to taxpayers for what they have requested earmark funding for. Therefore, this arbitrary system only benefits a specific group, not the general citizenry who have paid taxes that fund these projects. In 2009, individuals in congress spent $19.6 billion on earmarks.

EXCISE TAX or DUTY – A type of tax charged on certain goods produced in the United States, and is the tax on the production or sale of such goods. Taxes on gasoline, alcohol and tobacco are good examples of an excise tax. This type of tax is also called a "Sin Tax."

FASCISM – Perceives a nation as a single entity that binds people (citizens) together by ancestry, which is considered a unifying force of the populous. Fascists support unification and expansion of power and territory for their nation. Fascism is authoritarian in its political structure. It is usually a single party state controlled by a dictator.

FAIRNESS DOCTRINE (media) – The doctrine requires broadcasters using public airwaves to give equal time to opposing political views. Originally instituted in 1949 by the FCC and repealed in 1987. Considered by most to be anti-First Amendment since talk radio is dominated by conservative hosts and liberal talk radio draws few listeners.

FISCAL CONSERVATIVE – Advocates a reduction in overall government spending. Key to this philosophy is balancing the federal budget and deficit reduction. Fiscal conservatives have a strong belief in free trade, deregulation of free market, lowering taxes, and free trade. Pro-business; they believe in efficient, non-wasteful government, responsible government spending, and paying off national debt.

GERRYMANDERING – Drawing election district boundary lines for partisan advantage. This is a form of election fraud which violates the one voter-one vote fairness that redistricting is designed to preserve. Every ten years the U.S. Constitution requires a census to be taken and the results used for reapportioning both federal and state representative districts according to population.

HYPOCRITE – Someone who acts in an opposite manner to what they have stated. One who contradicts themself.

IGNORANCE – The general lack of knowledge, education, or awareness. A term first used in the 13th Century.

INDEPENDENT (political) – A citizen or elected person not affiliated with any political party. Independents generally have a centrist view between major political parties, or may have a concern for an issue not being addressed by any of the major political parties.

INTEGRITY – Doing what is right even under pressure to act otherwise.

INTELLIGENCE – An overall term describing many abilities of the human brain, including reasoning, solving problems, comprehension, capacity to learn, decipher and understand. Intelligence is measured as an average of these abilities.

KNOWLEDGE – The accumulation of fact, expertise, and skills acquired by a person through experience and education; the cognitive acquisition of data and facts.

LAISSEZ-FAIRE – The term used for the policy of allowing something to take its own course. Economically and politically is used to refer to government not intervening in the marketplace, and other aspects of society and personal life.

LIBERALISM (LIBERAL) – An ideology that individual liberty and equality are the most important political and social goals. Liberalism began as a movement for individual freedom. Liberals believe in the continuous improvement of society referred to as Progressivism. Liberalism emphasizes individual rights, free choices, and equality of opportunity for all members of a society. To do this, liberals advocate regulation of business and giving federal government ultimate power. Not bound by traditional or conventional ideas or values, they espouse new ideas in the name of progressivism. Liberalism became an ideology in the early 1800s and is associated with the *New Deal* of President Franklin D. Roosevelt, who brought on the concept of the *welfare-state*. Liberals are also termed *leftists* because of the left of center position they occupy politically.

LIBERTARIAN - A political belief that you should have the freedom to do what you wish, as long as it does not hurt or hinder others or take away their freedom. The only need for government is to make sure that people do not take away the freedoms of others; therefore, maximizing individual rights with minimal government.

MARXISM (MARXIST) – Political philosophy originally stated by Karl Marx and Friedrich Engels. Marxism is critical of capitalism and believes in social change, and usually started by a revolution. At its core is that class struggle is the pivotal element of social change. In Capitalism there are two classes: the Capitalists, termed the Bourgeoisie (who control the means of production), and the Workers (termed the Proletariat), who do not own the means of production and thus must work for the Capitalists for their survival. Marxism promotes the overthrow of Capitalism to replace it with a classless society, producing goods for direct consumption and not for profit, and distributing these goods in an equal manner. (See Socialism and Communism)

MODERATE (in American politics) – One who holds moderate views and beliefs. A moderate is considered a politician that holds the middle position, and that generally seeks a balance between the views of liberal and conservative issues.

MONARCHY – A government in which total power is vested in one individual who is the head of state. Traditionally this was a king or queen, which had absolute control over their subjects. A monarch may hold their unlimited power for life, until their abdication, or overthrow. It was a common form of government during ancient and medieval history, and was usually by heredity rule. At the writing of this book, over 40 nations have monarch rule, many are in the Middle East. In Europe separation of God and state ended in the 17th century, with the doctrine of the divine right of kings; "Divine Kingship." Absolute Monarchy existed in France until 1789, and Russia until 1917. The United Kingdom is a Constitutional Monarchy.

NANNY STATE – A term that refers to putting the government as a decision maker to determine for you what your best interest is. It is the perception and concern of government becoming too intrusive in controlling your personal life, and it becoming institutionalized as a common practice. Similar to the concept of a welfare state. Overt interventionist and regulatory policies of a state into families and the free market. Thomas Jefferson stated: "I predict future happiness for Americans if they can prevent the government from wasting the labors of the people under the pretense of taking care of them."

NATION STATE – A group of citizens that are part of a single political entity, usually a sovereign political state. Populations may be in the millions, they usually share common customs, history, and language. The United States is a nation state consisting of peoples from many cultures from other states.

NAZISM (NAZIS) – National Socialism of the National Socialist German Workers Party (NSDAP) under Adolf Hitler, from 1933 to 1945. Nazism is considered a form of Fascism. Nazism incorporated elements from both political left and right, and incorporated a combination of ideologies. Pivotal to their doctrine of nationalism was anti-communism, and adherence to traditional Aryan ethnic values and purity.

OLIGARCHY – Form of government with power resting with a small elite group of the society. This privileged group is usually considered royalty, military, or religious elite. Many oligarchies have been controlled by a family, which nurtures subsequent members to be heirs to the small power circle. Oligarchies have historically been tyrannical. (See Monarchy)

PATRIOTISM – A feeling and pride toward one's country; the love of and loyalty to one's country. Patriotism is a connection to the United States and fellow Americans through a shared culture, traditions, and history.

POLITICALLY CORRECT – Term applied to language, gender, culture, ideas, policies, and behavior to be respectful of, not offensive to any gender, race, culture, or specific group. As a political term it has been traced back to Mao Tse Tung's *Little Red Book*, of the People's Republic of China, a collection of quotations by Mao over his lifetime. By the 1960s the term had been adopted by the radical left.

PORK BARREL SPENDING (Earmarks) – Political slang for pet-projects by a legislator who uses tax payer money. A government appropriation or project only benefiting a specific district or area, or group, with jobs or improvements which gives unfair recognition to a representative, and therefore, his or her political popularity or constituent support. (See Earmark)

PROGRESSIVE (PROGRESSIVISM) - A political term referring to the ideology and party platform of promoting progress, change, improvement or reform by using government power to accomplish these changes. The term is contrary to keeping things the same, or changing them over a course of time. Progressivism is the belief in aggressive change, improvement or reform, as opposed to remaining status quo, or by measured incremental change. The use of government power to achieve change. (See Liberal)

PYSCHE – Is the whole being of a person; the cognitive energy in an individual that influences thought, feeling, behavior, and personality. The term is from Greek meaning "breath of life."

RATIFY – Term used to confirm, by giving your consent and approval.

REPUBLIC – A state in which the people have influence on its government. In republics that are also democracies, the head of state is elected by the people. In a presidential system, such as the United States, the head of state is also the head of government.

REPUBLICAN - Member of the Republican Party, one of two major political parties in the United States. Founded in 1854, is often referred to as the Grand Old Party (GOP), and is usually center to right politically. There have been ten Republican Presidents to the writing of this book.

SOCIAL CONSERVATIVE – Political and social ideology that government should emphasize and emulate traditional values, beliefs, and morals which have kept people civilized. A Social Conservative strives to preserve these traditions in present day society through civil law, politics and regulation. Traditional social values and morals are regarded as tried and true. This term became common during President Reagan's administration in the 1980s.

SOCIALISM – Economic theories politically and socially advocating public or state ownership and overseeing of the production and distribution of goods and services, and a society based on economic equality for all citizens. Socialist thought developed during the Industrial Revolution in response to the growth of private ownership in society, and was nurtured by such writings as those of Karl Marx. Marx promoted that socialism would be achieved through a "proletariat revolution" which would bring on a transition from Capitalism to Communism, the total elimination of class. (See Communism, Marxism, Nanny State)

STEREOTYPE – A simplified term referring to a person having similarities to a particular group, class, culture, or sub-culture. The term originates from Greek, meaning "solid impression." Although the use of stereotypes may be complementive or negative, a stereotype usually has been derived from a real situation, original characteristic, observation, or occurrence. Stereotypes can come and go in usage. When referring to someone who is untidy, a simple stereotype heard is that "he's a pig" assuming that pigs are always dirty. Stereotypes are heard socially as well as politically.

TOTALITARIANISM – A political system or state that exercises total power and control over the political, social, and culture of their subjects. A single party controls the government state-controlled mass media, with massive state oversight of the people, government and economy. Nazism relied on totalitarian government based on Fascist principles. Usually overseen by a dictator, Totalitarianism forces an entire population to one official state ideology. Although very similar to an Authoritarian form of government, a Totalitarian state is more all-encompassing, even controlling the social and political lives of its populous. The government goal is total control, and does not allow any independent organizations to exist. (See Authoritarian, Dictatorship, and Tyranny)

TYRANNY – A government where a single ruler has absolute power. Absolute power usually exercised unjustly and with only self-interest of the ruler. (See Authoritarian, Dictatorship)

WELFARE STATE – A term where the state assumes all aspects of social welfare services for every citizen; beyond just defense, criminal and civil justice, and regulations-- traditional guarantees of a sovereign state to its citizenry (rights given to each individual citizen of the United States by our Constitution and Bill of Rights). A precursor to the welfare state was the institution of social insurance by First Chancellor of the German empire, Otto von Bismarck. Early welfare states were Sweden and New Zealand in the 1930s. Welfare states are more prevalent in developed and economically stable nation states. A welfare state is usually accomplished through a combination of democracy, welfare and capitalism. During the Great Depression, under President Franklin D. Roosevelt's "New Deal" was the greatest American experience of social welfare in the nation's history. (See Nanny State)